The Four Steps to Freedom

UNF*CK
YOUR LIFE

I0542732

Christopher Canwell

RAMPAGE BOOKS

ISBN 978-1-9998722-4-3
eISBN 978-1-9998722-9-8

Rampage Books
www.rampagebooks.com

First Published by Rampage Books in 2023

Christopher Canwell has asserted his right to be identified as the author of this work in accordance with the Copyright, Designs, and Patents Act 1988.

About the Author

Christopher Canwell is a psychologist and author of the bestselling book *Atomic Attraction*. He works with clients around the world. For more information, please visit www.developattraction.com

Disclaimer

Throughout this book I have included many case studies that are based on people, events, and real-life situations. These case studies are all based to some degree on events and scenarios I have witnessed. All names, locations, and personal information have been changed for obvious reasons. Any similarities to other people or events are purely coincidental.

Table of Contents

Introduction

Every living creature wants freedom. A state of being we take for granted, freedom is more than just a way of life. The offer of freedom lies at the heart of every great myth. Freedom is the reason we strive for independence; it's why we start revolutions; it's the reason we start businesses and move across the world in search of new opportunities. Freedom is the reason humans are willing to risk life and limb for a better future. Whether you're looking to free yourself from terror, persecution, slavery, or simply want to choose what to do with your life, the search for freedom is humanity's most noble pursuit.

There are, of course, thousands of books that promise freedom, wealth, and prosperity. What makes this book any different? And, more importantly, what makes it worth your time? This book is designed to be a practical guide for change, inviting you to take a closer look at your life. What you see might disturb you or make you feel uncomfortable, and that's okay. All this book asks is that you stay honest and don't hide from the truth.

In a practical sense, when you apply the lessons in this book, you will see impressive results that go far beyond your expectations. You'll notice that the quality of your life improves: you'll sleep better, have greater peace of mind, be more energetic, and experience a greater sense of purpose.

Nevertheless, to get the most out of this book, you must have the confidence to examine your life with uncompromising honesty. This will be tough. I'm not talking about the type of honesty where your only obligation is to tell the truth, although that is important. Uncompromising honesty means accepting reality no matter how ugly or uncomfortable it might be. Only then, in a moment of stark exposure, can you find your true path and calling.

The famous Greek philosopher Epicurus believed that the purpose of life was to seek pleasure over pain. But if you avoid pain, especially emotional pain, you leave yourself with no room for growth. You get stuck, and life becomes difficult. Life is often tough, and it's only natural to search for happiness in new clothes, new cars, new relationships, better jobs, tastier food, and luxury holidays. But no matter how many possessions and experiences you buy, you cannot buy happiness. This book, however, is not about seeking happiness. It's about destroying the old to create the new: new opportunities, new possibilities, and a new way of life.

Many people are trapped in jobs they don't like, in relationships that bring them little to no satisfaction, and lifestyles that cause them stress and despair. In quiet moments when we have time to reflect, we long for change, but life seems to get in the way. We have bills to pay, family members to take care of, and groceries to buy. Who has time for change?

With each year that passes, our internal struggles become more intense, pulling us further away from where we want to be. For some people, this feeling is accompanied by a sense of doom, while for others it's more subtle—a nagging worry that they're heading in the wrong direction, unable to find the right path. And while you struggle, you continue to dream—of wealth, prosperity, love, and happiness, but, more than anything else, for freedom. The freedom to choose where to go, what to do, who to love, where to live, and what to do with the precious time you have left on this earth.

Some people want to change careers, some people want a chance to find true love, some people want fame and fortune, and some people want nothing more than the freedom to wake up without the sound of an alarm clock piercing the morning air. With that said, any creature, whether human or animal, that is restricted or trapped is a slave. And while you might not be bound by ropes or locked in chains, it's easy to become trapped in a slave mindset—a mindset that keeps you stuck, limiting your growth and potential.

Many people remain stuck in a slave mindset their entire lives. The fact that you're reading this book is, at least, a sign that you're aware, or about to become aware, of your situation. Awareness is the turning point. The point where a dangerous, exciting thought enters the mind: Can you change your life?

Work, relationships, spiritual well-being, the present, and the future are all areas of life you can change, all areas of life you can destroy. But for change to take place, something must give, and sacrifices must be made. In other words, destruction is needed for change to take place.

Paradoxically, destruction is sometimes constructive, opening up new paths on which to travel. At other times, destruction is devastating, laying waste to everyone and everything in its path. If you mishandle destruction, it's easy to find yourself enslaved, once again, in a life of despair. Successfully navigate your way through destruction, however, and something magical happens: you move away from slavery, beyond destruction, into a state of creation. A state where new possibilities open up. A state where you have the chance to shape your destiny and create the life you desire.

The creator stage is the start of a new beginning. Cultivating a creator mindset, however, is a challenging step on the path to mastery which is often fraught with difficulty. But what is mastery, and why is it something we should aspire to? Mastery, in this case, refers to mastery of the self, for only with complete mastery can you achieve complete freedom.

This book aims to guide you from a life of suffering and servitude to a life of freedom and opportunity. If you feel lost and directionless, this book offers you a roadmap to change. If you feel haunted by your past and unable to move forward, this book will help you become unstuck. And if you're looking to become the best version of yourself, this book can provide you with the tools you need to unfuck your life. Each of the four stages outlined in this book serves a critical purpose. These stages are slavery, destruction, creation, and mastery.

The first stage, slavery, refers to the state of being bound or held captive by our limiting beliefs, negative thoughts, and situations that hinder our progress. While slavery is no longer permitted, most of us are still slaves. We are slaves to our emotions, relationships, work, attachments, addictions, beliefs, and possessions.

The second stage, destruction, involves breaking free from the chains of enslavement. This is often a painful process that requires us to let go of old, unproductive beliefs that no longer serve us. The destruction stage can be challenging, but it is a necessary step on the path to freedom.

Rising from the fire of destruction, you have the chance to make a new life for yourself, creating new paths and beliefs to change the direction of your life. The third stage, creation, is marked by experimentation and a willingness to try new things. Creation is an exciting stage that enables us to change the direction of our life and open ourselves up to a world of new possibilities.

The final stage, mastery, is characterized by a deep sense of confidence and purpose. If you want to take control of your life and set yourself on the path to freedom, you must learn to master yourself and your environment. Mastery represents the ultimate goal of personal growth and development. And while we might attain mastery in certain areas of our life, in other areas we might remain stuck and feel helpless. It is my hope that in difficult times this book can offer you guidance and a clear path forward.

I

SLAVE

"The bird born in a cage thinks flying is an illness."

– Alejandro Jodorowsky

T HE MOMENT WE'RE BORN and come into this world, we're enslaved. From a young age, we're taught how to be good, law-abiding citizens. Society, culture, school, and family impose rules on us that tell us how to think, how to behave, and how to live. While a degree of domestication is required to maintain harmony, too much domestication stifles the spirit and enslaves the mind. Society programs us to be good little children, then good domesticated adults. When we're good and follow the rules, society rewards us. When we're bad and break the rules, we're punished. By the time we become adults, we no longer need to be told how to behave because we naturally censor and control our behavior to conform to society's expectations. We pretend to be someone we're not in order to fit in. Now, stripped of all resistance, we slot into the system like a tiny cog in a big machine.

We grow up, go to school, work, pay taxes, get married, then have children who grow up and repeat the same process all over again. If we deviate from this norm, we're criticized and shamed. But what about your dreams, your aspirations, and your plans for the future? It's become increasingly common for people to ignore their dreams to maintain the status quo. We lie to ourselves to look good. We pursue wealth and material possessions to make us feel better about ourselves. We struggle through relationships, even if a relationship is toxic, because it's the "right thing to do." And we punish, judge, and blame ourselves if we can't meet society's expectations.

When we think of slaves, we often imagine half-naked men and women breaking their backs, working in a field to the sound of a whip cracking above their heads. This is the most notorious form of slavery, where one person takes another person against their will and puts them in chains. Because the Slavery Convention of 1926 labeled slavery a crime against humanity, many people assume that slavery no longer exists. There are, however, more slaves walking the earth today than three hundred years ago.

Slavery is illegal, but most of us are still enslaved. We are slaves to our emotions, relationships, attachments, addictions, beliefs, and possessions. The woman caught in a toxic relationship and the man languishing in prison for assault have one thing in common—they are slaves to their emotions. Slavery is insidious because it sneaks into our life and takes hold of us. Only when we find ourselves caught in slavery's crushing grip do we try to escape or lie down and wait for death to arrive.

The woman who refuses to leave her abusive partner enslaves herself by staying in a relationship that acts as a prison. Why does the woman stick around? Is it the deluded belief that the relationship will one day get better? A chance to fix her partner? In this situation, hope blinds the woman to the truth.

When a circus trainer captures a baby elephant, the elephant struggles and resists. The elephant is wild and powerful, which makes taming it even more difficult. So what does the circus trainer do? They chain the elephant's leg to a tree so it can't run away. The elephant is trained to believe that it can never break the chain around its leg, no matter how hard it tries.

With time, the elephant grows weary. After several weeks, the circus trainer removes the chain from the elephant's leg, replacing it with a thin piece of rope. The rope is delicate and weak, yet the elephant doesn't try to escape. The elephant is now psychologically enslaved. Having grown up with the belief that the rope is unbreakable, the elephant can't understand that with one simple lunge, it can snap the rope and walk free.

Humans are not too different from elephants. We're born into this world a blank slate. Then, slowly, over time, we imprison ourselves. We grind it out in jobs we dislike, we trap ourselves in toxic relationships, we struggle to buy things we can't afford, and as life gets more stressful, we succumb to a variety of addictions in a desperate attempt to numb our pain. It's safe to say that compared to all other animals, humans are the least free and most restricted. We imprison our bodies in the same way we imprison our minds. And if we aren't enslaved by other people, we find a way to enslave ourselves.

The Emotional Slave

"None are more hopelessly enslaved than those who falsely believe they are free."

– Johann Wolfgang von Goethe

Picture the following scene: A man is driving in heavy traffic when another car cuts in front of him. Enraged, the man blasts his horn and screams profanities. He can't believe it. How could someone do that? Furious, he beeps the horn again, this time a long, drawn-out blast. The man feels a momentary sense of relief before his anger comes rushing back. *I'm stuck in traffic for over an hour, and this guy has the nerve to cut me off? Goddamnit! People have no respect. Nobody respects me, not my wife, not my kids, not my boss, not even this guy. Fuck!*

At that moment, the traffic starts to move. The man hits the accelerator and pulls out beside the white sedan that cut him off. He glares at the driver, a slick-looking businessman talking on the phone. The driver in the white sedan looks over and gives him the finger. The man explodes. *That's it! Not only does this guy cut me off, he gives me the finger? Who the hell does he think I am, some sucker who'll just take it? Well, not anymore!* In a fit of rage, the man yanks the steering wheel to one side, slamming his car into the white sedan.

An hour later, the man is sitting in hospital. *What was I thinking? I sent that guy to emergency with serious injuries. I'm sitting in hospital, my car's a write-off, and I can't afford to buy a new one, let alone fix this guy's car. Will I lose my license? Probably. Will I go to jail? There's a good chance.* The man puts his head in his hands and sighs. *How could I be so stupid? If only I could turn back time. Why was I so angry? What's wrong with me? I should've just let it go.*

While this man is undoubtedly guilty of road rage, he's also a victim. He's a victim of his own emotions. Any time you lose control and do something you regret, you become a slave to your emotions. Suppose someone disrespects you or goes out of their way to insult you. In that case, your thoughts will naturally lead to feelings of anger and resentment. In psychology, this is called *amygdala hijacking*, where the emotional part of the brain overrides the rational part. If someone is physically or verbally abusive, there's a good chance their amygdala has been hijacked.

Take Alice and Richard, a couple struggling to stay together after being in a relationship for the past two years. Alice and Richard love each other and enjoy each other's company. There's only one problem: Alice doesn't trust Richard. She hasn't caught Richard doing anything wrong—yet. He hasn't lied to her, cheated on her, or been abusive towards her. But something in Alice's mind tells her not to trust Richard. She thinks he must be hiding something. She's trusted men before, and they've all let her down. Why would Richard be any different? And with that, Alice's thoughts spiral out of control, making her feel more and more insecure. *Is he cheating on me? Did he lie to me? How can I trust him?*

In this profoundly emotional state, it's only a matter of time before Alice destroys the relationship. Even though Richard has done nothing wrong, he's judged guilty by a jury of toxic emotions. Alice has allowed her emotions to distort her perception of reality, inadvertently putting a death sentence on their relationship. This highlights one undeniable fact: If we don't control our emotions, our emotions will control us. This is not to say that emotions are useless or unimportant.

Emotions are a vital part of who we are and how we experience life. While emotions can make life sweeter, they can also cause havoc and destruction. We see evidence of this when our emotions put us in self-sabotaging situations. While it's true that our emotions can guide us in a positive direction, they can also derail us. So how can you prevent this from happening?

The best way to deal with unruly emotions is to get ahead of them before they bring chaos into your life. Thought creates emotion. Any time you notice negative emotions stir within you, stop and ask yourself if these emotions are valid? Just because you feel an emotion doesn't mean it is there to help you, as emotions often put short-term ego gratification ahead of everything else. While our emotions often work to serve our ego, they frequently do so at the expense of our safety and well-being. This results in emotional slavery, which stops us from progressing and traps us in a life of discomfort and self-sabotaging behavior. It's for this reason that you must make a conscious effort to control your emotions before they overwhelm you and disrupt your life.

The Psychological Slave

"Freedom and slavery are mental states."

– Mahatma Gandhi

The people-pleaser, the nice guy, the goody two-shoes, the defeatist, and the prude are all examples of psychological slaves. Consider the child who's raised to put the needs of other people first. They are taught to give their toys to other children, share their ice cream when another child doesn't have any, and never speak their mind in case they upset other people.

Over time, the child constructs the belief that their needs aren't important. This is self-imposed slavery at its worst. No longer free and expressive, the child learns to put other people's needs first. The child grows into an adult and feels more and more undervalued and underappreciated, which gives rise to powerful emotions like anger, fear, sadness, despair, and depression.

When you put other people's needs ahead of your own, you become a slave to those people. You might think this is a noble sacrifice, a worthy tradeoff, but there's nothing noble about psychological slavery. The psychological slave seeks validation above all else, for without validation and acceptance, they feel worthless. Thus begins an endless cycle of validation and approval seeking, which can never be satisfied. And much to the slave's frustration, the harder they try to win people over, the more they trap themselves and diminish their value.

Some of the most stressed-out people in the world are people-pleasers and nice guys. Even though this form of stress is self-inflicted, nice guys and people-pleasers continue to put other people's needs first to the detriment of their own well-being. Human nature is such that the more you try to please people and get them to like you, the more they resent you and lose respect for you. Similarly, when you allow emotions like greed, fear, anger, and jealousy to control you, you set yourself on the path to self-destruction, for these emotions have the power to make slaves out of all of us.

For example, if you compare yourself to other people, you'll likely end up feeling less fortunate than everyone else. Why does the family next door have a nicer car? Why do they have a bigger house? Why do they make more money? And why does everyone else have a better life?

When you compare yourself to others, you psychologically trap yourself. There will always be someone who has more possessions, more money, and a bigger house than you. This is why it's futile to compare yourself to others. When you spend all your time looking up, you forget to look down and see all those who are less fortunate. You remain a slave to greed and envy as you measure your self-worth by how much you have in comparison to other people.

Many people find themselves caught in the grip of psychological slavery. Often, this enslavement is a product of a dysfunctional belief. There are times, however, when our psychological enslavement comes from interacting with other people. We become a target of the modern-day slave master. Three hundred years ago, slave masters captured large groups of people and forced them to work as slaves, but the modern slave master works in much more subtle and sinister ways.

Modern slave masters are the bullies, liars, abusers, manipulators, narcissists, and psychopaths of the world. These people want nothing more than to control, dominate, manipulate, and abuse everyone around them. You might wonder why someone would want to enslave another person? Indeed, taking away another person's freedom puts the very nature of freedom in jeopardy. As Abraham Lincoln once said: "Those who deny freedom to others deserve it not for themselves." But does a narcissist or manipulator care about such things? The answer is no.

Slavery is a repulsive concept to someone who values human life. But we must remember that narcissists, manipulators, and psychopaths thrive on power and control. These toxic individuals come from all walks of life. You will encounter them everywhere. The sweet old grandma whose greatest joy is manipulating family members, the angelic boy whose biggest thrill is abusing his playmates, and the friendly work colleague who conceals their desire for power behind a caring facade. These are just a few examples of toxic individuals you might encounter in everyday life.

If you're unfortunate enough to come across one of these individuals, you must keep your guard up because they want nothing more than to enslave other people. In essence, your happiness is their misery, and your despair is their joy. Any happiness or success you experience brings out the worst in these people. And any power they can take from you only serves to inflate their ego and sense of control.

Little does the toxic individual realize that in their insatiable desire to enslave others, they inadvertently enslave themselves. In the same way that a person who lies to others lies to themselves, a person who abuses others also abuses themselves. This might sound like a contradiction: how can you abuse yourself when you abuse other people? When you harm other people, you convince yourself that the world is a scary place full of abusive people. When you lie to others, you convince yourself that the world is full of liars. And when you manipulate and deceive people, the world becomes a dangerous and deceptive place where no one is trustworthy. All this leads to long-term damage, stripping away the ability to love and trust other people. Instead of living a life of joy and abundance, the slave master and the slave are bound together by fear, destined to live a life of perpetual slavery.

It's safe to say that fear has enslaved more people than any man or prison ever could. Fear is so prevalent and pervasive it's like a virus that infects the mind. In this respect, fear is the killer of dreams and destroyer of hope. For example, if you're too scared to quit your job and pursue your passion, it's not your job that's holding you back; it's fear of change. One interesting aspect of fear, however, is that it exists solely within the confines of the mind. Suppose you feel scared to leave the house because of all the negative headlines in the newspapers about crime and disaster. Once you give in to your fear and refuse to leave the house, you psychologically enslave yourself. You become a victim of fear.

Newspapers, social media, and constant background chatter place a tremendous psychological toll on the mind. You must be vigilant to protect yourself from dangerous mental clutter. Otherwise, you risk becoming overwhelmed by constant noise and fearmongering. Fear is like the boogeyman hiding in the closet. It's terrifying because you can't see it, but you convince yourself that it's there. Once you summon the courage to open the closet, fear evaporates and disappears. Fear lives and dies in the mind. You feel scared and believe your fears to be real when fear is nothing but an illusion created by the mind.

Suppose you analyze all the areas of your life where you feel frustrated. What stops you from improving your life? After some reflection, you might notice that the only thing holding you back is fear. It might be fear of failure, fear of change, fear of stress, fear of financial ruin, or fear of the unknown. Once you pinpoint and highlight the major problem areas in your life, you can start to overcome your fear one small step at a time.

People often wonder why they allow themselves to live in fear. They wonder why they allow fear to hold them hostage and prevent them from living the life of their dreams. This thought becomes all the more frustrating when you realize just how long fear has held you in its grip. While fear can prevent people from taking action, your belief system has the power to enslave you or set you free.

Most of our problems are rooted in childhood. If one girl calls another girl "fat" in the school playground, the insult is still fresh in the girl's mind twenty years later. Even when the girl grows up to be anorexic and skinny, she still can't erase the words "you're fat" from her memory. An insult thrown in childhood has fueled a poisonous belief that infects every moment of the woman's life. Every time she looks in the mirror, she tells herself, "I'm fat and ugly," when nothing could be further from the truth. The girl's truth and the truth of the world are vastly different, and her damaging self-talk continues to destroy her confidence with each year that passes.

Another example is the young boy whose teacher tells him he must have a learning difficulty after he fails a science test. The following year, the boy still can't shake the belief that there's something wrong with him. He has accepted what his teacher said was true and no longer believes that he can learn anything. He might as well give up. Because of this damaging belief, the boy fails school, then bounces around from one minimum wage job to another, all the while telling himself, *I'm stupid, I'm a fucking idiot, I'm dumb.* The young man grows up with the crippling childhood belief that he can't learn anything and there's something wrong with him. Thanks to one misguided message from a careless teacher, the young man is psychologically enslaved. His health and future well-being now hang in the balance.

The Relationship Slave

"Self-deception can lead to self-destruction."

– Aesop

So much of life revolves around relationships: with family, friends, and co-workers. While relationships can bring great joy and happiness into our lives, they can also be a source of great sadness and frustration. If you're not careful, it's easy to become stuck in relationships with toxic people, emotional vampires, and abusive, controlling partners.

In contrast, positive people are nourishing in the same way that sunlight and water nourishes a plant. There will be moments, however, when you notice poison and rot creep into your life in the form of negative people whose presence suffocates and restricts your growth. If you wish to survive and flourish, you must cut toxic people out of your life. Otherwise, their negativity will continue to infect you, leading to atrophy and decay.

Consider the person trapped in a toxic relationship. The thought of leaving the relationship never enters their mind. Because of this, they become a slave to their relationship. Trapped in this mindset, leaving the relationship is more terrifying than staying. Ever hopeful, they hang on to the wonderful memories, even though they are few and far between. All the while, they feel trapped, suffocated, and deprived of love.

People who find themselves stuck in toxic relationships often dream of escape, yet they feel powerless to make a change. There are so many unknowns. What will happen if they leave the relationship? Things might be bad, but they could be a lot worse, they tell themselves in a desperate attempt to soothe their anxiety. They hold out hope that one day everything will change for the better.

They believe their situation won't last forever. They pray that something or someone will come along and save them. They don't know what that something or someone is, but they pray for it anyway. It could be death, it could be an accident, it could be a dramatic change in their partner's attitude or personality. They lie to themselves that everything will be alright if only they hold out a little longer. In psychology, this is known as the *sunk cost fallacy*.

The sunk cost fallacy suggests that the more time you invest in someone or something, the harder it is to walk away. To avoid giving in to the sunk cost fallacy, it's always a good idea to pay close attention to your emotions. People often dismiss their emotions and push their feelings to one side. This is particularly the case with men, who often prefer to ignore their emotions at the expense of their own well-being. And, in an equally devastating way, women often sacrifice their emotional needs to maintain peace in a relationship. Ignoring your emotional needs is damaging because it keeps you stuck in denial and emotional enslavement.

How much of your life are you willing to sacrifice by putting other people's needs first? This question becomes all the more important when dealing with emotional vampires. An emotional vampire is a person who drains your energy, time, and emotions. You'll know you're in a relationship with an emotional vampire when you feel tired in their presence. You're mentally and physically drained and often can't even summon the energy to mount an effective escape.

Emotional vampires don't drain their victim's blood to enslave them, they drain their energy. Perhaps you're stuck in an abusive relationship. Perhaps your partner's an emotional vampire. Or maybe you find yourself stuck in a relationship with someone who doesn't care about you or pay attention to your needs. You're trapped in an endless web of lies and deceit. You want freedom, but you can't escape. You know all you have to do is walk out the door, and the abuse ends. Walk out the door, and you're no longer a slave. But why is it so difficult to open the door and walk away? The answer is simple: you're trapped by your emotions. The relationship slave finds themselves stuck in a relationship that offers no nourishment and slowly eats away at their soul. Like one of Dracula's victims, they are drained of life and too weak to escape.

On the surface, the relationship slave appears to be the only victim in a toxic relationship. Yet, on a deeper level, the abusive partner is also a slave and a victim. Consider the person who cheats. Often unhappy and dissatisfied, they seek intimacy with someone from outside the relationship. While deep down they know they're hurting their partner, in their mind leaving the relationship is more hurtful than cheating. To the outside world, this is selfish behavior. Yet, the cheating partner is also enslaved. They are enslaved by a relationship that makes them feel trapped. Even though this doesn't excuse their actions, it helps us better understand their self-sabotaging behavior. Instead of communicating honestly with their partner about what they feel is missing in the relationship, the unfaithful partner searches for escape in the most destructive way possible.

Suppose you feel trapped in your relationship, enslaved by your emotions and your partner. This might be the perfect time to reflect on how you came to find yourself in this situation. Do you want to be with your partner but find it difficult to be around them? Are you attached to your partner but feel as though you need to detach from them? Are you in love with your partner yet despise them at the same time? This dichotomy represents the dual nature of relationships: good and bad; dark and light; love and hate. In toxic relationships, however, there's more dark than light, more chaos than peace, and more dependency than freedom. Your relationship remains skewed towards the negative, for a truly loving relationship is neither suffocating nor restrictive—it is wholesome, loving, and free.

The Material Slave

"Greed is permanent slavery."

– Ali ibn Abi Talib

With the arrival of the Industrial Revolution, technology pulled millions of people from their farms to work in factories and sweatshops around the world. This work was often back-breaking, and employers paid workers next to nothing for their labor. This technological shift gave birth to an industrial phenomenon known as the "wage slave"—a term that describes workers who are paid just enough money by their employers for basic survival. Over time, the industrial economy continued to grow, becoming more efficient and profit-focused. In response, employees were forced to work longer hours for less pay in difficult and often life-threatening conditions.

Fortunately, times have changed, and working conditions have improved. But wage slavery still exists. Today, millions of people find themselves trapped in an endless cycle of work-eat, work-buy, work-sleep. The modern wage slave receives just enough money to survive and to make sure they come back to work the next day. Most workers don't earn enough money to leave their jobs without facing severe economic hardship. No safety net or support system allows them to break free and become self-sufficient. These are the true wage slaves of the world.

The employer/wage slave dynamic is so prevalent that most people have experienced wage slavery in one form or another. If you feel trapped in a job you dislike, if you can't afford to leave, or if you're constantly worried about being fired, you're a wage slave. It is not just poor and unskilled workers who find themselves in this situation. Wealthy, educated people can just as easily find themselves trapped in the same frustrating cycle.

While the poor, unskilled worker remains trapped in a cycle of poverty, the wealthy, educated worker is trapped in a cycle of debt and desire. The more possessions they covet, the more money they need, and the more they have to work. Their mounting bills keep them stuck on the nine-to-five treadmill. One of the key problems with modern work is that so much of it is debilitating. While the industrial economy has helped pull billions of people out of poverty, it has enslaved just as many. We are wage slaves, but it's hard to notice when working nine to five is considered normal.

Despite its prevalence, our bodies and minds cannot adapt to the nine-to-five routine. Consider that humans have evolved over millions of years to be one with nature and the environment. We now have more food than ever before, yet we're more starved of nutrients than at any other time in human history. We have never been so safe and comfortable, yet our bodies have never been so unhealthy.

The simple act of sitting down for hours on end has caused millions of people to suffer back pain, inflammation, and obesity. Does this sound like liberation? This state of being has become so common, however, that we no longer question its abnormality. Our bodies are weaker and more disease-prone than ever before. And our mental health and well-being is affected too: depression, loneliness, and anxiety are rife in the modern world.

At no other time in history have humans been so isolated, troubled, and overworked as they are today. This has brought us to the point where many people's lives are no better than a hamster spinning a wheel inside a cage, working paycheck to paycheck just to buy more possessions. This doesn't mean that work is pointless. Work is one of the most important aspects of life, and good work provides great meaning and value. Nevertheless, there is a difference between meaningful work and work that provides no value.

The worker who spends their days flattering their superiors to make them feel important; the worker who manipulates systems for their own gain; the pen pushers and box tickers who pretend to be busy but do nothing but waste their time and the time of others; and managers who create work for work's sake; all these people bring mass inefficiency into the workplace and prevent us from creating real meaning and value in the world. If we're not careful, low-value work can enslave us in a cocoon of false comfort as it steals our most valuable resource—time. Time for family, time for friends, time for health, and time for adventure. Time is always more precious than money.

Some people claim that money is the root of all evil, but money is simply a medium of exchange. We need money to buy food and put a roof over our heads. Money is not evil, but it does have the potential to corrupt and enslave. Just as buying possessions can enslave us, institutions and people who lend us money enslave us by expecting something in return. These expectations might include loyalty, a favor, or interest payments on a loan. If you chase money to buy things you don't need under the illusion that more possessions will improve your life, you expose yourself to the dark side of money and become trapped. This trap arrives in the form of debt, a house you can't afford, furniture you can't sell, or a loan that you struggle to repay.

While striving to own a better home and a nicer car can motivate us to work harder, owning these items often brings more misery than happiness. So often, wanting is better than having. Wanting a big house is better than owning a big house, and wanting expensive clothes is better than owning expensive clothes.

Dopamine, a feel-good chemical in the brain that regulates pleasure and motivation, plays a vital role here. With each new purchase, dopamine gives us a brief boost of exhilaration before tapering off, leaving us with a desperate urge to go out and buy something else. This doesn't mean that possessions and money are bad and do irreparable harm; we do, however, need to be careful not to become slaves to our possessions. Ultimately, it's how we think about money that matters.

Why is money so desirable? Beyond its fundamental purpose to buy goods and services, money can buy us the one thing we all crave—freedom. Freedom to live where we want, do what we want, and control our own time. Yet, despite these significant benefits, most of us don't use money to set ourselves free. Instead, we become a slave to money, trapped in a never-ending cycle of work, debt, and despair.

The Addiction Slave

"Man is born free and everywhere he is in chains."

– Jean-Jacques Rousseau

In the modern world, where stress, isolation, depression, and anxiety are so prevalent, addiction is there to fill the void, to seduce us with the promise of excitement and escape.

The Sirens of Greek mythology perfectly encapsulate the seductive nature of addiction. These mermaid-like creatures, who lived on an island in the Strait of Messina between Italy and Sicily, had voices so beautiful and seductive that passing sailors found themselves unable to resist their call. The sailors would steer their ships towards the sound of the Sirens, where their ships would crash and sink on the rocks hidden beneath the shallow water. Sometimes, the sailors would drown in the sea; at other times, they would make it onto the island, where they found themselves stranded without food and water. The sailors would soon starve to death as the Siren's song distracted them from hunting and foraging. Here, the myth of the Sirens is a metaphor for addiction.

Consider all the different types of addiction: alcohol, drugs, gambling, smoking, work, love, food, and TV, to name just a few. Most of us will fall victim to one or more of these addictions in our life. An addict can be rich or poor, educated or uneducated, old or young. Addictions don't discriminate. But they are always there, ready to pounce whenever tragedy strikes or we hit rock bottom. Addiction is poison disguised as a helping hand.

Like the Siren's song, addictions are seductive because they offer us a chance to escape from the drudgery and monotony of our lives, and to escape our sadness and pain. Addictions provide the false promise of peace and happiness. This is the deceptive nature of addiction. We all feel pain, and we all suffer. How we handle our pain and suffering, however, determines our fate. Do we turn to addiction to escape or find a more positive outlet for our emotions?

The drug addict working in a job they hate is no different from the alcoholic stuck in a miserable marriage. Both deal with their stress and disappointment by using addictive substances to drown their sorrows and numb their pain. The problem is addictions only exacerbate our pain and make us feel worse.

Addictions provide the illusion of escape and comfort. They provide momentary solace. And while we're caught in our addictions—drinking to excess, gambling our money away, and using drugs to numb our pain—they slowly take over our life and eat us from the inside out. Instead of finding escape and solace, we become lost to disease, poverty, and decay. And, if we're not careful, our addictions not only ruin our health, drain our wealth, and steal our time, they infect our relationships and leave us with nothing but despair.

The effects of slavery are, to this day, real and devastating. Slavery causes great suffering on both a conscious and unconscious level. When you find a moment to reflect, ask yourself whether you've experienced or are experiencing psychological, emotional, or addiction issues in your own life? If the answer is yes, you mustn't feel ashamed. It doesn't matter if you're rich or poor, healthy or unhealthy, young or old—enslavement touches all of us at some point in time.

If you remain stuck in a slave mindset, however, the relentless effects of stress, anxiety, fatigue, tension, and depression will continue to plague and torment you. Unfortunately, some people remain stuck in a slave mindset their entire life. You can recognize these people by the way they walk, stooped and bent, their faces sad and full of despair. Often irritable and downtrodden, the modern-day slave looks at the world with confusion as they try to figure out why everyone else is more prosperous and fortunate than themselves.

If you pay close attention, you'll notice millions of people sleepwalking their way through life with nothing to strive for and no hope in sight. According to the naturalist and philosopher Henry David Thoreau, these are the people who live "quiet lives of desperation." It's at this point, the point of desperation, that you must be prepared to face a brutal and profound truth: Nothing will change unless you're willing to set yourself on a new path. Fortunately, this is not as difficult or as traumatic as it might sound. The first step on the path to freedom is simple: You must become aware of your situation and the truth of your life. Only then, in a quiet moment of introspection, can you destroy those parts of your life that hold you back and keep you enslaved.

II

DESTROYER

"Every act of creation is first an act of destruction."

– Pablo Picasso

O F ALL THE STAGES mentioned in this book, the destroyer stage is the most critical, challenging, and difficult to navigate. For this reason, it's important to know about the many different types of destruction, whether destruction comes from an external event like a devastating earthquake or destruction is internal and personal, namely the destruction of the self. In this case, destruction is a form of emotional detox where you destroy negative attachments and dysfunctional beliefs, including letting go of the past and learning to release negative emotions.

Any person who's tried to change their life has, at some point, had to enter a destroyer mindset to create change and move past destruction on to creation. During this transition, there is a risk that the person might destroy themselves in the process. This is why the destroyer stage is so difficult to navigate. That being said, people from all walks of life manage to find a way through destruction into creation.

Business executives, single mothers, addicts, entrepreneurs, teachers, murderers, and saints all occupy the same destructive space. Good or evil, rich or poor, everyone wants change. The desire for destruction is so strong it echoes through history. We need destruction to lay waste to the old and make room for the new. Here, destruction can be used as a force for good or chaos. We see the chaotic desire for destruction in the story of the young man who dreamed of becoming an artist.

The year was 1908, and the young man spent his days drawing and painting around the streets of Vienna, one of the great cultural cities in Europe. Seeking nothing less than artistic greatness, the man applied to Vienna's Academy of Fine Arts. Unfortunately, the academy rejected the man's application on the grounds that he had a greater talent for architecture than painting. The young artist labeled this moment a crisis point and a "bolt out of the blue." It was at this point, a point of great psychological disturbance, that the young artist transitioned from a dream of creation to a dream of destruction.

No one could predict that this unremarkable individual would go on to create a level of destruction and suffering that was unprecedented in human history. To this day, you can see the man's paintings in private galleries and collections around the world—the infamous signature "Adolf Hitler" scrawled in paint across the bottom of each canvas.

We see examples of destruction throughout history. In the same way that it's easier to destroy a rainforest than it is to plant trees, it's easier to destroy life than to create it. While destruction brings death and ruin, it also opens up a path to rebirth and renewal. If you wish to move forward, you must first destroy harmful attachments, dysfunctional beliefs, and destructive behaviors. Creative destruction means destroying old paths that divert you away from reaching your full potential.

Does your job cause you stress and dissatisfaction? Are you trapped in a relationship that eats away at your soul? Do you find yourself surrounded by people who criticize you for no other reason than to make themselves feel better? On a more ethereal level, you might feel as though your life is moving in the wrong direction. You know something is wrong. There's an underlying sense of unease that won't go away. Even if you don't know where this feeling comes from, it's important to listen and pay close attention to your instincts.

Why do you feel uncomfortable? In this situation, your discomfort is necessary because it lights a fire within your soul and shines a light on your problems. Are you distressed? Are you upset with the state of your relationship? Do you feel as though you're heading in the wrong direction? Do you feel lost and directionless? Once you become aware of your situation, it's time to make a change. Destruction, in this case, must occur before change can take place.

Destroying Relationships

"The only risk in bondage is breaking free."

– Gita Bellin

When a person is deeply unhappy with their life, they often dream that death will come along and save them. For example, a person trapped in a loveless, toxic relationship might fantasize that they, or their partner, will meet with an unexpected accident. It is, of course, not death that the person longs for, but the death of the relationship. Death, in this situation, is the desire for change.

If we ignore our desire for change, our destructive energy is more likely to rush out in a blast of unchecked emotion. If we listen to our inner truth, however, we know it is the destruction of our life path, not life itself, that we crave. A person caught in the grip of a dangerous and obsessive love is a good example of someone trapped in a destroyer mindset, unconsciously giving in to their destructive impulses. And when it comes to love, dangerous obsession can lead to deadly consequences, as seen in the relationship between Dan and Rachel.

Dan is head over heels in love with Rachel, a woman who wants nothing to do with him. Dan has tried everything from writing love letters to buying gifts, but no matter how hard he tries, nothing he says or does can persuade Rachel to give him a chance. Without him even realizing it, Dan's love soon turns into a dangerous obsession. The more Rachel rejects him, the more Dan struggles to win her over and convince her that his love is real.

For as long as Dan can remember, he's only seen one path to happiness: getting married to Rachel and living happily ever after. Dan's felt this way for the past two years, and nothing anyone says can convince him otherwise. Unfortunately, with each day that passes, Dan's dream seems more and more out of reach. Dan's suffering is sharp and real. He feels a heightened sense of anxiety followed by a tightening in his chest every time he breaths. Even his heart hurts. Why does love have to be so fucking painful? Dan knows he must do something to end his suffering or die trying.

When one last valiant attempt to win Rachel over ends in rejection, Dan buys a gun and vows to end his life. He goes home and leaves a note on his bedside table: "My life is meaningless. I can't live without Rachel. I'm sorry." At that moment, Dan prepares to commit the ultimate act of destruction. But instead of destroying his unhealthy attachment to Rachel, Dan makes the tragic decision to end his life. His last curtain call, a final act to end his suffering.

This type of destructive behavior is common in people who are reckless and struggle to control their emotions. People often destroy themselves and those close to them as a way to end their suffering and restore balance to their lives. They act out their destructive fantasies when all they want is to end their suffering. In this case, a destructive impulse can be so powerful it can lead to either rebirth or death.

Sometimes we're aware of our destructive energy, while, at other times, our destructive energy lies just beneath the surface in the realm of the subconscious. We often see destructive energy come to the surface in people who cheat in relationships. Here, the unfaithful partner carries with them a subconscious desire to get caught because they know an affair will likely end their relationship, a relationship their subconscious wants to destroy. Cheating is a selfish way to end a relationship, but that has no bearing on destroyer energy which, unless controlled, expresses itself in the most direct way possible.

Whether a person uses their destroyer energy to end a relationship in a respectful or destructive way, the underlying desire is the same: a desperate need for change in a time of crisis. When destruction occurs, we feel free and liberated. We allow our emotions to rise to the surface, no longer stifled by dysfunctional beliefs and unhealthy attachments.

In this case, it is healthy to move forward on a path of creative destruction rather than mindless destruction. Destroying old paths, however, is not for the faint of heart. It's easier to stay in a bad relationship than it is to destroy a familiar way of life. While the coward stays in a lousy relationship, supporting a toxic environment, brave and honest people leave unhealthy relationships to forge new paths of love and respect.

Marco's story offers some insight into how a toxic relationship can spiral out of control and hold us back. For the past five years, Marco hoped that his relationship with Sofia would get better. But no matter how hard he tries to make the relationship work, the constant fighting and tension never goes away—it only gets worse.

Deep down, Marco wants nothing more than to end the relationship. Yet he feels as though he can't break up with Sofia because he doesn't want to hurt her feelings. He is also worried that giving up on the relationship now would mean he'd wasted five years of his life. *All relationships go through difficult times, it's better to be patient and try to make things work*, Marco tells himself every time he thinks about breaking up. As a result, he is unable to move forward.

Then, out of nowhere, Marco notices a festering anger building inside him. This feeling is unusual. Marco's anger isn't directed at anyone or anything in particular. It's just there, boiling beneath the surface. Marco feels confused because he doesn't understand where his anger is coming from. It isn't long, however, before the source of Marco's anger becomes clear.

After another fierce argument with Sofia, Marco experiences an overwhelming sense of rage and a sudden urge to lash out, to strike Sofia; not because he wants to hurt her, but because he wants their fighting to end. He wants to silence her. Marco's soul craves peace. His impulse to lash out is not a desire to inflict pain, it is a desire to restore balance and harmony. Yet there is no peace. Every time Marco and Sofia fight, Marco bites his tongue instead of using his destructive energy to express himself and create positive change.

As you can see, it's easy to become stuck and feel trapped if you prevent your destructive energy from expressing itself. The destruction of a relationship is difficult, especially if you're in love with someone and feel attached to them. And although destroying a relationship is never easy, it is an essential step to end unnecessary suffering and bring about change.

Take the example of Grace, a woman who feels uncomfortable whenever she meets up with Ingrid. Ingrid and Grace have known each other since college. And although Ingrid has not said or done anything wrong, Grace can't help but notice that she always feels uncomfortable around her. It's clear that Grace's instincts are trying to tell her something: Her relationship with Ingrid doesn't feel right.

Then, one day, an incident occurs that sheds light on the source of Grace's discomfort. She gets promoted at work and discovers that Ingrid is anything but happy. While Grace receives messages of support from friends congratulating her, Ingrid says nothing. Instead, she ignores Grace for several weeks. Later, at a social event, Ingrid tells Grace that her promotion is "meaningless" and that "pretty girls with limited talent get promoted all the fucking time." Grace was right to feel awkward around Ingrid, who was clearly jealous and unsupportive. Her friendship with Ingrid is neither authentic nor genuine. And if Grace doesn't take steps to dissolve their friendship, Ingrid's jealousy will continue to infect her life, causing psychological harm and disruption.

Sometimes people who claim to be our biggest supporters are, in fact, enemies in disguise. Do the people closest to you have your back? Can you trust them? Do they support and encourage you on your journey through life? Or do they hold you back and try to stop you from progressing? Even family members and close friends can hold you back, offering little more than judgment and criticism instead of help and support.

The moment you become aware of this dynamic, you must use your destructive energy to end the relationship, otherwise it will prevent you from moving forward. Now is a good time to think about the relationships in your own life. Ask yourself which relationships are supportive and which relationships are harmful?

It doesn't matter if you destroy a bad relationship with elegance or brutality. It has to happen to allow you to move forward and create new relationships with people who care about you and support you. Suppose you fail to take action and remain stuck in a relationship that is toxic and debilitating. Your association with toxic people will continue to poison your soul as long as you interact with them and keep them in your life.

Destroying Attachments

"The root of suffering is attachment."

– Buddha

We don't just form attachments to people, but to beliefs, traditions, objects, possessions, places, and outcomes. While some attachments are healthy, other attachments hold us back and prevent us from moving forward. In relationships, we might become attached to the image of a person instead of the actual living, breathing human being. In terms of possessions, we might become attached to the idea that more possessions bring more happiness. And at work, we might attach to the belief that a better job or promotion will lead to more respect and status.

In Buddhism, detachment means recognizing that there is nothing to attach to, for everything is temporary and impermanent. This idea conflicts with Western beliefs that prioritize achievement and wealth above all else. In the West, we believe that every time we get a shiny new possession, like a new phone or luxury car, our lives will improve until we reach a point of ultimate satisfaction. Once you get these possessions, however, it soon becomes clear that any satisfaction is fleeting, and any emotional or spiritual problems that existed before still remain.

Buddhists believe that attachment leads to suffering. Thus, the fewer attachments you have, the less suffering you are likely to experience. Adam's story illustrates this point. Adam is a restless man in his forties. Hungry for adventure, he's just made the difficult decision to start a new life in a different city.

The moment Adam starts packing, seeing all his possessions piled up on top of each other, he begins to feel overwhelmed. There's furniture, cutlery, electronic devices, clothes, shoes, sports equipment, books, magazines, multiple TVs, a sound system, his grandparents' furniture, paintings, and a spare mattress. The simple thought of moving everything makes Adam feel tired. He can't imagine fitting all this stuff into his new apartment. Although it would be easier to sell his possessions or give them away, Adam is reluctant to leave anything behind.

After mulling it over for a couple of weeks, Adam decides to put his belongings into storage. *That way, I can always come back and pick them up later*, he tells himself. The moment Adam leaves his old life behind, however, and moves into his new apartment, he notices that he doesn't give his old possessions a second thought. He doesn't miss them, and he doesn't think about them.

Adam wonders why he made such a big deal about leaving his possessions behind. This is the paradox of desire: wanting is better than having. Adam was reluctant to let go of his grandparents' furniture and other sentimental items because he thought he would miss them. Instead, Adam discovers that his grandparents' memory is with him wherever he goes. His memories are, in fact, a part of him and not tied to his possessions.

Research shows that buying possessions brings us little in the way of happiness. We are, in fact, prone to grow bored of them the moment they are acquired. Instead of buying possessions, buying experiences brings us more satisfaction and happiness. This holds true even if an experience turns out to be disappointing or sour, such as a scary flight or spooky hotel. Bad experiences are useful because they provide valuable learning experiences and make the most memorable stories.

Destroying Beliefs

"If it can be destroyed by the truth, it deserves
to be destroyed by the truth."

– Carl Sagan

Cassie had looked up to Greg since the moment they met. Not only was Greg smart, but he had all the qualities Cassie believed she was missing in herself. Greg was hardworking, ambitious, single-minded, and most appealing of all, he believed in himself. He oozed confidence. Their relationship was built on love and respect—a happy marriage between two people who care deeply for one another. Because Greg was doing so well in his IT career, he often took it upon himself to give Cassie advice. "You should tell your boss to give you a pay rise," he'd tell her. "Don't stay in the same job too long, it's not good for your career."

"What career?" Cassie would shoot back. "I work reception, book meetings, and make coffee." Cassie wished she had a career, but that would have to wait. She didn't even have a college degree. Why would anyone want to hire her? If only she had a quarter of Greg's confidence, things might be different. *I'm pretty much useless*, Cassie told herself. *The only thing I'm good at is baking and making jam.*

Around six months later, Cassie went to the doctor and received some unexpected news. She wasn't sure whether the news was good or bad, but she felt excited. When Cassie told Greg she was pregnant, he froze, coffee raised, the mug resting on his lower lip as though the news had somehow paralyzed him.

"What are you going to do now?" he asked, squinting over his coffee. "I mean, what are you going to do for work?" Before Cassie had a chance to respond, he added, "We need the money."

"I don't know," Cassie said. "I'm as shocked as you are."

Greg sighed and stared out the window. "It's good news— yeah, it's good news," he said, rapping his fingers on the table, trying to convince himself.

For the next two months, Cassie stayed home, reading baby books, baking, and making jam. She considered this good practice for her new role as a mother. Cassie made all sorts of jam: strawberry, apricot, Naval Pazham, blueberry, and marmalade—all based on old recipes passed down by her grandma.

Much to Cassie's delight, when anyone tried her jam, their faces were a sight to behold. First, there was the look that said, "Okay, I'll humor you. I'll try your jam." Then, after popping a spoonful of jam into their mouth, there came a look that was hard to describe, a look that said, "Wait a minute, what is this?" It was a look of unexpected delight.

The jam was free, but that look was priceless; it meant everything to Cassie.

Cassie's jam was so popular that her friends kept telling her she should sell it instead of giving it away. Cassie appreciated the compliments but knew her friends were only trying to be supportive. Still, it was nice to hear. When Cassie told Greg that her friends thought she should open her own shop, he shot her a look. "Selling jam?" he scoffed. "There's enough jam in the world, just look in the supermarket."

The moment she heard the words, Cassie felt hot tears run down her cheeks. She knew she wasn't special, and she didn't have much in the way of talent, but it hurt to hear those words coming from the person she loved most.

The following day, Cassie woke up angry: angry that Greg didn't believe in her, and angry that he didn't support her. Why was he so dismissive? Why does he think so little of me? Sure, she was mad at Greg, but Cassie was also mad at herself. Furious that she'd never, for a moment, had the courage to believe in herself. Cassie went into the kitchen and did what she always did when she got upset, she cooked up a large batch of jam. And while she waited for the jam to set, Cassie stuck a label on an empty jar and wrote: "Blood Orange Marmalade—$3.50." It was the first time Cassie had put a price on something, let alone something she had made.

Running on fumes of anger and indignation, Cassie took a photo of the jam and sent it to her friends.

That evening, Greg walked through the front door, a big smile plastered across his face. "Hey, I just had a thought," he said, hanging his coat on the rack. "Forget about your old job. Once you have the baby, you can get a better job somewhere else." Cassie couldn't hold it in; her grin lit up the room. "I knew you'd be happy," he said. "All that sitting around doing nothing must be driving you crazy."

"Look at this," Cassie called Greg over and opened her laptop, turning the screen to face him. On the screen, her account showed twelve orders for blood orange marmalade.

"You've got to be kidding," Greg said, double-checking the screen. "You're selling to your friends?"

"I made more than forty dollars."

"No, you didn't."

"What do you mean?" Cassie replied.

"You forgot the cost of the ingredients and the cost of the jars. You think you made forty dollars, but you'd be lucky if five dollars of that was actual profit. I told you, you're not cut out for business," Greg said. Cassie looked at Greg, trying to read what was going through his mind. Greg straightened and stood up. "What, now I'm the bad guy?"

"Who cares if I only made five dollars, can't you be happy for me?"

"Sure I can. I just don't want you to embarrass yourself."

"How is it embarrassing?"

"It's just weird, that's all," Greg said as he strolled over to the fridge and pulled out a beer, popping the lid with unnatural speed.

"Why can't you support me? Just once."

Greg took a deep breath. "Look, I don't want you to be disappointed, that's all. I care about you. I love you."

Three months later, Cassie walked into the same apartment, only this time she was alone. Greg was gone, along with all of his belongings. He had only forgotten to take his coffee mug, which stood out, large and grotesque, in the corner of the kitchen cupboard. The mug's cartoon beaver scowled back at Cassie with the printed words "Dam It All!" echoing a thought she'd whispered to herself a thousand times.

Cassie surveyed the scene and pressed a hand to her stomach. A kick. Her baby. *How long had he been planning to leave? And why? What had pushed him over the edge?* Cassie tried to think back over the past couple of months. Everything had happened so fast. She remembered posting the marmalade photo. That wasn't the first sign of trouble, but it was significant. It was the first time she had believed in herself. The first time she'd taken a leap of faith.

Despite Greg's dismissive attitude, her jam sold well, maybe too well. Within the month, Cassie had more than two hundred orders. When she told Greg about her small success, he said nothing. No, "Well done." No, "That's amazing." Instead, he went to the fridge and grabbed another beer. He drank a lot that month.

The month after that was September . . . what happened? Cassie racked her brain. September was the month everything changed. The month she started questioning her beliefs: *I'm not smart enough; I'm too stupid to make money; I don't have any skills; I don't have any value in the world.* Could her friends be right? Was her jam really that good? Did she have talent, even if that talent was only a talent for making "crushed fruit with sugar," as Greg liked to call it.

In September, Cassie made two thousand dollars. When her friend Laura suggested she learn more about the business side of things, Cassie jumped at the idea, absorbing everything she could about sales and marketing. The following month, Cassie made two thousand dollars in just two weeks. Was that why Greg left, or was it because she was now making slightly more money than him? He should have been happy. The money was good for them, and with a baby on the way . . . Cassie ran her hand over Greg's coffee mug. Maybe it was her lighthearted comment that made him snap: "You should quit your job; we can team up and make jam together."

"And work for you?" Greg snorted in reply. "Go to hell." The harshness of his words stung her, but at that moment, Cassie was finally able to see things clearly: Greg was only happy when he had power over her. He was all bluff and bluster. The moment she spread her wings, he got scared and ran away. *Unfucking believable.* Cassie pulled the mug from the cupboard and dropped it in the trash. Now, instead of feeling sad, she felt relief. For the first time in her life, Cassie believed in herself, and that feeling was worth more than seven years of marriage.

On our journey through life, we pick up certain beliefs and assumptions. We develop expectations and grow into comfortable patterns of behavior. Along the way, we create beliefs that become a part of who we are. Some of these beliefs are positive, others negative. Because ideas spread like wildfire from one person to another, it's common to see the same beliefs and assumptions in different people around the world.

Some common beliefs include: I should be married by a certain age; I should own my own house; I should have my first child before I'm thirty; I need a degree to become successful; I'm not worthy of love; I'm always unlucky; I never get what I want; people are untrustworthy.

People often make incorrect assumptions about themselves and other people. At worst, we jump to conclusions and assume that everyone is out to get us. In less sinister but equally harmful ways, we form judgments and limiting beliefs that restrict our growth and personal development. For example, you might have been taught that it's shameful to stand up for yourself and be assertive. Over time, you come to believe that assertiveness equals aggression. You bury your needs and focus on other people's needs instead. You grow up with the belief that other people's needs are more important than your own. But as you'll soon discover, you can only bury and suppress your needs for so long.

When our thoughts and assumptions don't measure up to the standards set by society, we feel ashamed and repress our emotions. Suppose you continue to bury your needs and desires. In that case, you suffocate your spirit, which eventually leads to depression and anxiety. When you fail to bring your needs into the light, where they belong, your body takes an emotional hit.

While everyone has a public face to some degree in order to meet societal standards, these masks prevent us from revealing our true selves. Our authentic self remains hidden and stays buried. To live an authentic life, we must destroy our social mask piece by piece. The more you chip away at your social mask, the easier it is to live a meaningful life.

While everyone wears a social mask to some degree, putting on a different face to meet societal standards, social masks prevent us from revealing our true selves. Instead, our authentic self remains hidden and stays buried. To live an authentic life, we must destroy our social mask one fragment at a time. Destroying your social mask liberates you and moves you one step closer to freedom. The more you chip away at your social mask, the easier it is to live a meaningful life.

You can start to remove your social mask by questioning your assumptions and limiting beliefs. For example, a false assumption might be the belief that you're unworthy of love. Many people tell themselves that they're worthy of love, yet deep down, they feel unworthy and unlovable. In this situation, it's tempting to use positive affirmations to build yourself up. Positive affirmations, however, won't work, no matter how creative or elaborate you make them.

You can't stand in the mirror and tell yourself, "I'm unique and amazing and deserve love," if you don't believe this statement to be true. Positive affirmations like this don't work because they conflict with the truth. If you're lacking in some area or have work to do, you must be brave enough to admit this to yourself. This is your truth. You can lie to others, but you can't lie to yourself. As the Russian author Dostoyevsky said, "Lying to ourselves is more deeply ingrained than lying to others." When you look at your life, you must be honest about where you stand and your place in the world. If you wish to liberate yourself, you must first embrace the truth, no matter how ugly the truth might be.

People often try to suppress their needs, which can stem from feelings of guilt, shame and embarrassment about who we are and what we want. In reality, there's nothing shameful about your desires. Instead of trying to suppress your desires, you must bring your needs into the open, no matter how dark or disturbing they might be. Once you've identified your limiting beliefs, you can work towards destroying them, which, in turn, will allow you to create a new set of beliefs that support your long-term goals and desires.

Destroying Old Paths

"In the waves of change, we find our true direction."

– Unknown

All your thoughts and actions have led you to where you are today. Thus, if you're not happy with your life, this means that your thoughts and behaviors have set you on the wrong path. How do you know if you're on the wrong path? If you constantly feel anxious or depressed, there's a good chance you've walked too far down the wrong path. Depression and anxiety are warning signs. It's your body telling you something is wrong, that you need to change course and follow a new path. When you think about your relationships, friends, workplace, hobbies, home, environment, how do you feel? Does one area of your life make you feel more depressed or anxious than another? If the answer is yes, this is a good indication that you need to find a different path.

Many people feel guilty when they think about changing their life. What will my friends and family think? Am I selfish, putting my needs first? Whatever the cause of your guilt, remember that, in situations like this, guilt is of little value. Guilt is an emotion that has the potential to weigh you down and hold you back. You must, however, never feel guilty for destroying something that needs to be destroyed.

The Japanese samurai and philosopher Miyamoto Musashi once said: "Do not regret what you have done." Once you decide that it's time for change, you must move forward without regret, for it's right to destroy that which no longer serves you. You must embrace destruction, not shy away from it. When handled the right way, destruction is satisfying because it moves you closer to your true purpose, even if this means throwing your life into momentary chaos.

For example, if you're the type of person who feels depressed in cold, dark, gloomy weather, moving to a warm, sunny climate is a good practical solution. Yet while you know this move is essential for your long-term health, you struggle to make the move a reality. There are so many attachments holding you back and you're reluctant to make a bad move or wrong decision. You ask yourself if you can really leave your old life behind? Despite your fear, you know in your heart of hearts you must destroy the path you're on to overcome your depression.

Suppose you notice that you always feel stressed out and depressed at work. Your energy levels are low, and you have no motivation. You know you must leave your job to move onto a more productive path. When your internal environment (thoughts, beliefs, assumptions) and external environment (work, relationships, home) no longer serve you, it makes sense to change course.

Are your thoughts holding you back? Do you notice that when you talk, you only tell people what they want to hear? Do you do whatever you can to make other people happy, sacrificing your happiness for the sake of others? If the answer to these questions is yes, ask yourself, are you living for yourself or others? At this stage, you have two choices: remain trapped in a slave mindset or transition to a destroyer mindset.

If you keep your feelings bottled up without expressing yourself, you will become blocked. Instead of being directed outwards, your destroyer energy focuses inwards. This has a devastating effect on the body, as your emotions, now trapped, turn your body into a simmering volcano that can explode at any moment. People often try to repress their feelings by putting the needs of other people first. They give the impression that they're calm, relaxed people, then shock everyone when they explode in a fit of rage, laying waste to everyone and everything in sight.

Once you enter a destroyer mindset, it's tempting to unleash the full force of your destroyer energy, wrecking everything in your path. But honesty is always a more efficient method of destruction. The truth will set you free, but to live with honesty, you must know yourself and speak your truth. You must have the courage to tell people what you want and how you feel, leaving no doubt about your intentions and desires, even though some people might not like it, especially those who prefer to live in denial. Genuine honesty is beautiful and refreshing. It clears away the old and ushers in the new. Honesty has a way of setting us on the right path, especially in our relationships with other people.

Suppose you continue to live in denial and refuse to destroy those parts of your life that need destroying. In that case, you will remain stuck in a state of depression, anxiety, and frustration for as long as you stay on the same path. Change is a necessary component of life. If you keep repeating the same behaviors, thoughts, and mistakes that led to your enslavement in the first place, nothing will change. You'll remain stuck until you summon the courage to accept the truth and break free.

Shiva, the Hindu god of destruction, is worshiped for his ability to protect people from ignorance and delusion. In Hindu scripture, ignorance and delusion stand in the way of divine enlightenment. That is why Shiva is also the god of rebirth, representing creation and destruction in the great cycle of life. When you destroy the old and create the new, you set yourself on the path to freedom and enlightenment.

It is only your attachment to negative thoughts, people, and beliefs that hold you back. Turning your back on toxic people, dysfunctional beliefs, and destructive environments opens the door to a new life and ends unnecessary suffering. Destruction is something to be embraced, not feared. You must be willing to destroy paths that no longer serve you, for only in the flames of destruction can you rise like a Phoenix from the ashes and create the life you desire.

III

CREATOR

"In a time of destruction, create something."

– Maxine Hong Kingston

I N THE EARLY 15TH CENTURY, a girl was born on a small farm in rural France. During this time, France was at war with England, fighting over a claim to the French throne. This long, drawn-out conflict, known as the Hundred Years' War, saw years of fighting accompanied by long periods of peace and stability. With almost the entire war fought on the battlegrounds of France, the English employed a crippling scorched earth policy that shattered the French economy and devastated the land.

The French military, unable to achieve any significant victories for over a generation, was now on the verge of defeat and about to surrender when a little farm girl appeared on the scene with a vision from God. That girl was Joan of Arc. She claimed that two saints appeared before her in her father's garden to deliver a message: Drive the English out of France and help install the Dauphin on the French throne.

Historical records allege that on the way to the French court, Joan said, "I must be at the king's side . . . there will be no help for France if not from me. Although I would rather have remained spinning wool at my mother's side, yet must I go and must I do this thing, for my Lord wills that I do so." The entrance of Joan of Arc marked an astonishing turnaround in The Hundred Years' War. Up to this point, having suffered one humiliating defeat after another, the French seemed to have little choice but to surrender.

Some sources claim that Joan's appearance was the only source of hope for the French. It was perhaps for this very reason that the French king made the drastic decision to place an illiterate farm girl at the head of his army—an army Joan would lead to a sudden and unexpected victory against the English.

Over the years, a lot has been said about Joan of Arc. In France, she is viewed as a saint who turned the tide of war and saved the nation. The English, however, claimed that Joan was a witch, and when they eventually caught up with her, they burned her at the stake. Other historians have argued that Joan was given to flights of the imagination and suffered from mental illness.

Despite what people might say, one thing is certain: Joan gave the French hope in a desperate fight against an enemy that had ravaged France for more than a generation. With nothing more than a dream and a vision, Joan of Arc was a source of light in a time of darkness. Indeed, her vision was so powerful she created a new path for her country and liberated the French from oppression. Joan's story is a testament to the power of the human spirit and our ability to change the course of our lives, even under the most challenging circumstances.

All humans possess a unique and powerful gift—the ability to create something out of nothing. From the Taj Mahal to the electric light bulb, the most famous creations in history started out as simple ideas. Masterful creations can be large or small. They can be a work of art, a personal project, or the start of a new business. No matter the scale, all creation originates from a single idea. Everything you see around you, from the car that you drive to your favorite movie, originated in the mind of a person just like you. Make no mistake, there's a life force, a spirit, and an energy that lies within you, waiting to be unleashed upon the world.

The human mind, which contains approximately eighty-six billion neurons, is an organ of incredible power and complexity. It is capable of both astonishing creation and great destruction. Using nothing more than the power of your imagination, you have the ability to forge a new reality. You can create prosperity out of nothing. You can imagine new and beautiful creations, and you can change the entire course of your life using only the power of your mind.

When used as a force for good, the mind can create wonderful works of art, make incredible discoveries, and create endless opportunities. When used as a force for evil, however, the mind can just as easily become an agent of destruction. We see this in the example of Hitler and other tyrants throughout history who sought power and destruction over peace and prosperity.

When Hitler rose to power, he did so with a vision of rebirth and renewal—a vision that seduced an entire nation. Hitler's vision, however, turned out to be corrupt. Instead of rebuilding Germany, he destroyed his country and set the world on fire. Hitler was a destroyer, not a creator.

Both Napoleon and Hitler started out as visionaries who forged compelling dreams of liberation for their respective countries. Over time, these dreams turned into nightmares of destruction and death. Every person who's achieved greatness or made an impact in the world had a dream, and every person who freed themselves from slavery had a vision. Visions and dreams can appear from out of nowhere, or they can be created and cultivated with conscious effort.

When you create new beginnings, you destroy that which you leave behind. You transform your thoughts into positive energy—energy to change your life and impact the world around you. You must be careful, however, to harness your destructive energy for creative purposes, not chaos and ruin. When you move from a path of destruction to creation, you take part in the eternal process of rebirth and transformation. This transformation encompasses all forms of change from close-minded to open-minded, weak to strong, unhealthy to healthy, intolerant to tolerant, and enslaved to liberated.

Creating New Beliefs

"Your beliefs become your thoughts."

– Mahatma Gandhi

If you want to change your beliefs, you must first change the way you think. Similar to the way blood and cells regenerate within the body, you can transform your life using the power of your mind to forge a new reality. Consider Matt, a sensitive, compassionate man who feels restless whenever he thinks about his life. Matt's relationship brings him no joy, his work is laborious, and he seems to pick up a new injury or illness every month.

On top of this, Matt feels as though he's being swept along by forces outside his control. He believes he can't get a new job because no employer would want to hire him, and he believes he can't get in shape because being overweight is part of his DNA. To get through the day, Matt tells himself: *It's okay, one day everything will be alright.* This thought is Matt's mantra, which he repeats to himself every time he gets depressed.

Matt dreams of the day when a benevolent stranger will appear from out of nowhere and offer him a job working in a place where people appreciate him. While Matt continues to dream, he repeats his mantra: *It's okay, hold out a little longer, one day everything will be alright.* From this example, you can see that Matt has yet to create a new set of beliefs that will allow him to change direction and create a new path with a more promising future. Until then, Matt remains stuck in a slave mindset, unable to move forward.

Albert Einstein once said that insanity was "doing the same thing over and over again and expecting different results." Like Matt, if you keep thinking the same thoughts and performing the same destructive behaviors, you're destined to remain stuck, unable to develop or move forward in life.

Did you know that the average person has approximately twelve to sixty thousand thoughts running through their head every day? And 95% of these thoughts are repetitive. Out of all these thoughts, how many do you think are harmful and destructive? Research suggests that up to 80% of all thoughts are negative. If you continue to tell yourself, with passive repetition, that one day everything will be alright, you do nothing to encourage change or create a new path. Instead, you burden yourself with a counterproductive mindset. You give up control of your life and put yourself at the mercy of other people, random life events, and circumstances outside your control. To create a new path, you must encourage new thoughts and behaviors that move you in the right direction.

The French Emperor Napoleon once said: "Imagination rules the world." Your imagination is both powerful and infinite. One of the major problems holding people back is a reluctance to start a new journey and give up their old way of life. We refuse to give up old habits and unproductive ways of thinking, we refuse to destroy the past, and we become attached to harmful behaviors and dysfunctional beliefs.

We cling to the path we're on, regardless of how useless or destructive that path might be. Instead of creating a new set of beliefs, we support our dysfunctional beliefs with negative self-talk. When we examine our thoughts and become aware of our self-talk, we're often shocked to discover how much is negative and toxic.

Take a moment to think about how you talk to yourself and how you think about other people. If your self-talk is negative, you'll notice that harmful thoughts flow through your mind in a stream of toxic consciousness: *I'm stupid; I'm such an idiot; I can't do anything right; I'm unlovable; I'm so ugly; I'm not interesting or fun to be around.*

While most of our thoughts are directed inward, we also direct many of our thoughts outward: *I hate that person; this place is horrible; everyone's so stupid; that person is ugly; I fucking hate people.* Your thoughts are converted into real-world energy—energy that not only shapes your inner world but your outer world as well. It's common for people with a lot of negative self-talk to develop crippling anxiety and depression.

Naturally, when you think about yourself in a negative light, this inflicts wounds on your soul and shatters your confidence. If you think negatively about other people, you can't help but feel as though other people must also think the same way about you. Once you become aware of your negative self-talk, you can take active steps to destroy your old way of thinking.

Suppose you grew up with the belief that "being assertive is shameful." In response, you come to believe that assertiveness equals aggression. This makes you scared to reveal your true feelings and stand up for yourself. To overcome this, you should first destroy the belief that assertiveness equals aggression. This belief can be dismantled by changing the way you think about assertiveness. Instead of upholding the belief that assertiveness equals aggression, you can choose to reframe how you think about assertiveness. Were you told to "stop being aggressive" as a child because it hurt other people's feelings? Were you, in fact, being aggressive or just standing up for yourself?

A good way to dispel the notion that "assertiveness equals aggression" is to examine how you came to develop this belief in the first place. Perhaps an adult once told you to "stop being aggressive" when you upset another child. Even though this happened twenty years ago, you might examine how the statement "stop being aggressive" instilled in you the belief that being assertive was shameful and wrong.

Perhaps the adult who told you to stop being aggressive was trying to protect their child, a child who bullied other children. Now, with the passage of time, you can see the situation more clearly. You were simply standing up to a bully and trying to protect yourself. You can use this thought as a springboard to take a closer look at your entire belief system. Are you scared to stand up for yourself because you don't want people to think you're selfish and mean? Bringing your lack of assertiveness into the open is important if you wish to destroy this limiting belief. Only then, after destruction has taken place, can you create a new set of beliefs that better serve you.

An excellent way to create new beliefs is to replace your old thoughts with new, vibrant thoughts. For example, you might believe that you can't learn a new language because you don't have a talent for it. To challenge this limiting belief, you can replace the thought, *I can't learn a new language,* with the following belief: *It's easy to learn a new language. I just need to be interested in the language and put in enough time and practice.*

Learning how to create new thoughts and beliefs is essential for growth and development. Right now, your beliefs might bring you nothing but misery and dissatisfaction. But this is no reason to remain stuck on the same path. A person who's socially anxious and scared to meet new people is a good illustration of this point. Instead of repeating the same destructive mantra that they are scared to meet new people, they need to destroy their old beliefs and create a new belief such as, *"Most people are friendly, and I enjoy talking to people whenever I get the chance.*

Similarly, suppose you want to start a new company but believe that most businesses fail. In that case, you can replace this limiting belief by telling yourself: *Even though I feel nervous starting my own business, I'll feel much worse if I do nothing and let my dreams go to waste.*

Regret is one of the worst feelings in the world. Regrets have a way of haunting people. *I wasted so many years in terrible relationships; I wasted my life in dead-end jobs; I could've done better; I could've tried harder; I should've followed my passion; I should have loved more; I should have had more adventures.* These are just a handful of regrets expressed by people around the world.

If you're suffering from a bad case of regret, it's possible to erase those feelings by creating a new set of beliefs that allow you to move forward by encouraging self-reflection and personal growth. For example, you might tell yourself:

Although I've experienced many failures, my failures are not a waste of time as long as I learn from the experience. My failed relationship was a blessing because it taught me what I want and don't want in a partner. And even though I haven't traveled as much as I would have liked, had I done so when I was younger, I might not be as adventurous as I am today.

If you obsess over the past, it's because you have yet to absorb and process the important lessons it provides. The past, with all its trauma and painful memories, is there to teach us a lesson. Take Alison, whose high school memories are just as painful today as they were fifteen years ago. Alison, an extrovert by nature, now spends most of her time alone, avoiding people and social situations.

Over the years, Alison's social anxiety has spiraled out of control, becoming more debilitating by the day. And in those rare moments when Alison believes her memories have begun to fade, another traumatic event from the past pops into her mind, sending her into another downward spiral. Unfortunately, the past will continue to haunt Alison until she understands that her memories are there to teach her a lesson. If Alison is to find peace and move forward, she must first confront her painful memories and learn the lessons they contain.

First, Alison must accept that she played a part in her own victimization. This is a hard truth to accept. True, Alison was bullied by two girls in high school, two girls she considered close friends. Still, if Alison is honest with herself, she knows that these two girls never respected her; they weren't her friends. Instead of seeing herself as a victim, it's more constructive for Alison to turn her painful high school memories into a valuable learning experience.

In Alison's case, she was too trusting towards people she thought she knew well. She also ignored all the warning signs and refused to stand up for herself. While Alison works through her traumatic memories, she might discover that there are people in her life, friends, and colleagues, who continue to take advantage of her whenever she doesn't stand up for herself.

There are two lessons to be learned in this situation: Alison should be less trusting towards people she doesn't know; and she should stand up for herself whenever people try to take advantage of her. Once Alison internalizes these lessons, her painful memories can be put to rest. She is now in control of her past and no longer its slave. Sometimes, all it takes is a small adjustment in the way you think to become unstuck.

Like Alison, Courtney is a woman trapped in a slave mindset. She is a single mother, struggling to pay her bills while living paycheck to paycheck in a small, one-bedroom apartment. Throughout the day, Courtney's mood fluctuates from stressed to the hilt to barely functional. Unfortunately, this situation is an all-too-common scenario in today's world.

Courtney worries that she can't take care of her baby. She worries that her landlord will one day evict her from her apartment. She worries that she won't have enough money to buy food next week. And on top of this, Courtney struggles to hold down a minimum wage job as a cashier in a grocery store. If you were to dive deep into Courtney's mind, you would discover that 90% of her thoughts and worries revolve around money. *Why am I broke? It's not fair; Why does everyone else have money except me? I can't make money because I don't have any fucking connections; the game's rigged; rich people don't want poor people like me to make money; I'm fucked; you need money to make money; I can't make more money because I don't have time to get a better job; no one will hire me because I didn't do well in school.* Courtney repeats the same thoughts to herself from the moment she wakes up to the moment she goes to bed, week after week, month after month, year after year. Courtney's thinking all but guarantees she remains stuck in a never-ending state of financial slavery.

Like the saying goes: "Change your thinking, change your life." To change her life and improve her financial situation, Courtney must first destroy her old beliefs and start thinking differently if she is to end her financial misery. Of course, there's little point if her new thoughts are just as ineffective, such as: *I can make money like everyone else; I will be successful and get a better job; one day, I'll be rich;*

if I think I'm successful, I will be successful. These thoughts are artificial and contrived. Instead of creating positive affirmations, it's much more effective for Courtney to construct a new belief system around money and finance—a belief system that nudges her towards wealth and prosperity.

The modern world is full of information and knowledge, making it easier than ever to create a new belief system. This could include the following positive thoughts: *Money is a reward for providing a service or something of value; working smart is more effective than working hard; all prosperity begins with belief; the universe is abundant; money flees from those who pursue it the most.* This is why money can seem so elusive. Money is not elusive; it is simply a reward for helping people. The more people you help, the more the universe rewards you. No one, including Courtney, can hope to liberate themselves unless they change the way they think and create a new belief system.

Creating New Paths

"If you can't find a way, create one."

– Manmohan Rathi

During World War II, amidst all the horror and chaos, a Nazi spy living in Poland destroyed his belief system for the benefit of humanity. The spy's name was Oskar Schindler. Schindler was a German businessman who worked for the Nazis, and, like Hitler, he cultivated a destroyer mindset. When Germany triggered World War II by invading Poland, Schindler saw an opportunity to profit from the invasion. He planned to set up a factory in Krakow using free Jewish labor provided by the Nazis. The Nazis would support him, and setting up the factory would be easy. The plan was perfect and provided Schindler with the perfect opportunity to make easy money.

Indeed, Schindler was a man who embraced a hedonistic lifestyle, seeking pleasure and comfort above all else. He was an alcoholic, a womanizer, and a ruthless businessman masquerading as a spy. But as the war dragged on, Schindler experienced a psychological disturbance. Disturbed by the brutality of the Nazis, Schindler made the unexpected decision to save as many Jews as possible.

If the Nazis discovered Schindler's plan, they would execute him for treason. But the threat of execution was nothing compared to the inner turmoil raging inside Schindler. Side with the Nazis and enjoy a life of prosperity, parties, women, and wealth; side with humanity and face danger, anxiety, stress, and the threat of execution. Initially stuck in a destroyer mindset that focused on greed, Schindler made the difficult decision to create a new set of beliefs focused on sacrifice, integrity, and love. As a result, he saved approximately twelve hundred Jews from the gas chamber.

What Schindler accomplished was no mean feat. When you move onto a new path, you'll invariably meet a great deal of resistance along the way. Even when you want to change the direction of your life, there are people out there who want you to remain stuck because it makes them feel less threatened. Some will try to hold you back out of jealousy and envy, others because they fear losing you and getting left behind. Anytime you try to change your life, you must expect resistance from both yourself and other people.

You'll notice similar patterns of resistance across all kinds of relationships. Someone might realize that it's better to be single than remain stuck in a toxic relationship that causes endless suffering. Yet, they encounter resistance from their partner, close friends, and family as they attempt to end their relationship. Their partner, terrified of letting go, will do anything they can to keep the relationship alive. In situations like this, you must choose the right path for you, not the path other people want you to follow.

Let's revisit an earlier example. When Cassie wanted to quit her job and start her own jam-making business, she was both excited and nervous at the idea of striking out on her own. Whenever Cassie thought about quitting her job, she felt energized and inspired. Imagine Cassie's surprise when she discovered that her loving husband seemed reluctant to help her. In fact, he did the opposite.

Greg spent most of his free time trying to convince Cassie to stay in her nine-to-five job, repeatedly telling her, "We can't afford to lose the paycheck." Cassie couldn't understand why the man she loved wouldn't support her. The answer was simple: Greg was threatened by her ambition. He worried that one day Cassie would be more successful than him, and he would lose power in their relationship.

On your journey through life, you'll come across many obstacles and people standing in your way. The boss who doesn't want to promote you because they're scared you'll rise above them and wield power over them. The friend who doesn't want you to succeed because they're worried you'll outshine them. And the family member who tries to limit your freedom because they don't want you to slip out from under their control. You must create strict boundaries with people who try to restrict your growth. This is a critical step if you want to gain control over your life.

Suppose you feel a continual sense of dissatisfaction and frustration. An uneasy tension that lurks just beneath the surface and won't go away. At times like this, you must pay close attention to your feelings. Are you in a place where you feel inspired and energized? Or are you surrounded by resistance and people trying to block you? Perhaps you notice that some of your friends don't respect you. In that case, it might be time to create a new set of friendships with people who appreciate and support you.

Similarly, if you work in a low-paid job with few benefits, ask yourself, *Is this the right path for me, or is it time to find a job more worthy of my talents?* When you experience a cocktail of negative emotions, ranging from dissatisfaction, frustration, depression, anger, and anxiety, your internal alarm is trying to tell you that there are issues in your life that need to be resolved. These issues can either be physical, emotional, or spiritual.

Whenever you feel disturbed by your emotions, you must pay close attention. This is especially true if negative feelings linger too long or become chronic in nature. This is your body and mind telling you that something is wrong—it's time to make a change. If you ignore your emotions, no matter how dark or distressing, you ignore an essential warning system in your body.

Naomi's case illustrates what happens when you ignore your internal alarm. Naomi is a struggling artist who's been living in the same city for the past twelve years. Every morning, she wakes up and feels depressed about the state of her life and where she lives. When Naomi goes to work, a feeling of discomfort follows her to the office where she works as a bookkeeper. Naomi knows something is wrong. She's uncomfortable with her life, her work, her environment, and the people around her. Whenever Naomi feels overwhelmed, she tells herself the same thing she's told herself for the past twelve years: *Even though life is stressful, this city is full of opportunity, and it's the best place for me to launch my artistic career.*

After twelve years, Naomi is still waiting for that opportunity to arrive and her career to take off. Instead, the city seems to bring nothing but tension and discomfort into Naomi's life—a feeling that lingers like a parasite under her skin. Naomi is at a crossroads. Does she stay and hope that things get better, or does she make the tough decision to create a new life somewhere else? One thing is certain: until Naomi leaves the city she's called home for the past twelve years, her depression and anxiety will continue to linger, telling her that change is not only preferable, it's necessary.

Creating new beliefs and thoughts is an essential part of our development. Most people only harness the full extent of their creative powers after a great psychological disturbance or seismic event rocks their world. This can be triggered by the end of a relationship, a sudden financial crisis, an unexpected illness, or a near-death experience. Although psychological disturbances are upsetting and often traumatic, they can provide us with an incredible opportunity for growth if handled the right way.

A psychological disturbance has the power to force us onto the right path through immediate and rapid destruction. As we've touched upon already, this is a crucial aspect of change, for only after destruction has taken place can you build something new. While most psychological disturbances arise from unexpected events, they can be simulated by focusing on those parts of your life where you feel the most pain.

Many people shy away from negative emotions to avoid discomfort, even though negative emotions are often trying to guide us onto the right path. Focusing on the pain points in life makes it easier to see where life needs improvement. Instead of ignoring the warning signs that your body sends you, it's much more effective to lean into your discomfort and focus on the source of your pain, whether it's work, relationships, financial problems, your living environment, or your physical and mental health.

Paul, a dissatisfied young man working in a mundane office job, is experiencing his own form of internal discomfort. For as long as Paul can remember, all he ever wanted was a chance to work in the film industry, writing and directing movies. When Paul told his parents he wanted to go to film school, they tried their best to discourage him from working in an industry with "bad career prospects" and a "low chance of success." Instead of going to film school, Paul's guidance counselor persuaded him to study business instead.

While studying for a business major in college, Paul noticed a feeling of discomfort creep into his life. During marketing lectures, Paul's mind would drift off, and he'd think about his one true passion—film. On top of this, Paul spent most of his free time watching movies, reading screenplays, and talking to like-minded friends about the movie industry. Every time Paul attended a business class, he knew, in his soul, he was in the wrong place. But without the support or courage to pursue his passion, Paul continued to grind it out in college, doing the bare minimum to graduate.

After college, Paul decided to look for work in the film industry. With newfound passion and determination, he scrolled through various job sites, looking for work in a low-paying industry with almost no permanent employment. It was all contract work. *I guess I've got to start at the bottom, then work my way up*, Paul thought. He wanted to pursue his passion, but he was practical and knew he needed to make enough money to pay rent and put food on the table.

With this in mind, Paul took the first job he could find in the marketing department of a large computer company. Within a week, he knew he was in the wrong place and the wrong job. And, once more, that heavy, uncomfortable anxiety, the same feeling he had in college, crept back into his life. Paul's discomfort was his body's way of begging him to change course, but he had bills to pay. So Paul did what he always did: He pushed his dream of working in the film industry to one side and continued in his dead-end job.

Paul watched the years roll by, and six years later, he was still stuck in the same job. All those years had taken a toll, and Paul was now a shell of his former self. He struggled to wake up, was often late to work, and when he got there, he did the bare minimum. After work, Paul spent his time daydreaming of another life—one where he dared to live with courage. Paul knew as long as he stayed in the same soul-destroying job, his feelings of anxiety, depression, and regret would continue to plague him.

At this point, in a moment of deep discontent, Paul fell ill and was admitted to hospital. By the time Paul was taken into the emergency room, he was in severe pain. His body was shaking, on the verge of death. It didn't take long for the doctors to realize that Paul's appendix was about to burst. The next day, as Paul lay in bed recovering from surgery, he felt a sudden and unexpected change come over him. It was as though something had shifted inside his mind. Little did Paul realize he was undergoing a psychological disturbance.

Lying immobile in hospital, Paul knew he had no choice but to quit his job and pursue his dream. Even if pursuing his dream meant taking a severe pay cut, starting all over again, and struggling to pay the bills. Paul knew he had to change the trajectory of his life or die with regret. The moment Paul left the hospital, he began to look for work. After an intense two-month search, Paul was hired as a script reader, reading and analyzing screenplays for a small, independent production company.

On his first day at work, Paul noticed something incredible: His stress and anxiety had all but evaporated. Sure, he'd taken a step down in terms of money, but that didn't matter. Paul had never felt happier. He no longer struggled to wake up in the morning. Instead, he jumped out of bed with passion and purpose. The anxiety and depression that had plagued him for so many years was now nothing more than a distant memory. Paul's path and purpose were, for the first time, in perfect alignment.

Find Your Truth

"Truth is not for comfort, it's for liberation."

– Sadhguru

You cannot be comfortable if you bury the truth. While you might try to trick yourself into believing that you're happy or content, you can only delude yourself for so long. You know deep within your soul whether you're headed in the right direction or stuck on the wrong path. All you have to do is listen to your emotions. Do you feel troubled and listless, or do you feel energized and inspired? If you fail to acknowledge the difficulties in your life, insignificant problems can soon spiral out of control.

People often ignore problems because they don't want to admit that something is wrong. But anyone who's ever tried to bury their emotions, no matter how dark and uncomfortable, knows they can only suppress their emotions for so long. It's only a matter of time before your emotions demand recognition. When you reflect upon your past behavior, you might discover that you're more selfish, vindictive, angry, and jealous than you would like to admit. Still, if you look closer, you might also discover that you're more creative, generous, and courageous than you know.

If you try to bury your authentic self, you become fractured, and, as a result, so does your life. To prevent this from happening, you must acknowledge your emotions and dark desires, even if this makes you feel uncomfortable.

Along the way, you might encounter a series of psychological disturbances as you uncover traumatic events and memories that you wish to forget. In addition, you might also uncover parts of your personality that disturb you. But you mustn't shy away from this experience. You should encourage this process and work to bring your true, uninhibited self into the light. Suppose you notice a side of your character that makes you feel uncomfortable, such as jealousy, anger, envy, or vindictiveness. In that case, it's better to acknowledge your dark emotions than try to dismiss them altogether.

Rafael's story is a good example of someone struggling to deal with their emotions. Rafael has noticed that he's started feeling resentful towards other people. These feelings are uncomfortable and confusing for Rafael, who prides himself on being a nice guy. *If I really am so nice*, he wonders, *why do I feel so fucking upset all the time?* The truth is, Rafael's nice-guy persona is just an act—an act that traps him into putting other people's needs first.

When Rafael is kind and polite, he's horrified to discover that people often take him for granted. They mistake his kindness for weakness. The problem isn't that Rafael is nice;

the problem is that he is deceiving himself. He pretends to be nice because he thinks that is what people expect of him. As a result, Rafael struggles to maintain the social mask which conceals his true personality.

Rafael buries his emotions for weeks, sometimes months, at a time. Thus, it's no surprise that Rafael's destructive energy is desperate to come out, to explode, to eradicate his fake, nice-guy persona. In this example, Rafael's destructive energy expresses itself as resentment, rising up like an immune system attacking a virus. If Rafael wishes to gain the respect he craves, he must first find the courage to open up and show his true self to the world. Only when Rafael finds the courage to stop living for others and start living for himself can he restore balance to his life and get the respect he so desperately craves.

The moment you enter a creator mindset, there's a good chance you'll notice some uncomfortable feelings stir within you. When this happens, you might recoil and reject what the psychiatrist Carl Jung famously referred to as the "shadow self." This describes those parts of our personality that lie hidden in the shadows, that we bury and conceal from the outside world. It might surprise you to discover, however, that many impulses we consider dark and unwelcome are, in fact, there to guide us and set us free.

Anytime you suppress your feelings and desires, your life will feel inauthentic and half-lived. Suppose you buried your creativity as a child because a parent or teacher told you that artistic skills were a waste of time. But no matter how hard you try to ignore your creativity, it is a part of you that can never be silenced. This is your true self. If you deny the truth in a vain attempt to look good in the eyes of society, the only person who suffers is you. If you run from the truth, it will continue to haunt you and make your life miserable.

Humans are masters of delusion. We delude ourselves by ignoring the truth; we delude ourselves in relationships; we delude ourselves into living a certain way; and we delude ourselves when it comes to making simple career decisions. For example, you might try to convince yourself that you want to be an investment banker because it's prestigious, and it gives you a chance to make a lot of money. Yet you have no interest in the world of finance and would love nothing more than to do something creative. Nevertheless, your belief system tells you that creativity is a waste of time and a fast track to poverty. The key, in situations like this, is to listen to your inner truth. What do you want? What do you desire? What feels right? Knowing what you want is half the battle. Once you know what you want, you must have enough courage and conviction to choose the right path.

The ancient Romans worshiped Janus, the god of new beginnings, transitions, and endings. Janus was arguably the most important Roman god because he also represented the cycle of life. The cycle of life is played out in both profound and subtle ways, influencing everything from the rain and the harvest to our attitudes and beliefs. When we move away from beliefs that no longer serve us, we witness the destruction of guilt, fear, shame, and self-loathing. The moment you create a new path for yourself, you experience a newfound freedom and acceptance of both yourself and others.

Sometimes, you might need to take baby steps towards freedom, and, at other times, you might need to take a dramatic leap to change your life. Don't be upset if change doesn't take place overnight. Sometimes you must untie the rope that binds you one knot at a time. While some knots are easy to untie, others require more effort and persistence. No matter how difficult your situation, imagination coupled with action grants you the power to forge a new reality—a reality where you take control of your life and master your destiny.

IV

MASTER

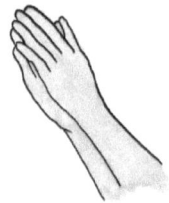

"Control your own destiny or someone else will."

– Jack Welch

ROUND 111 BC, the Roman army captured a young Thracian boy and forced him into slavery. The boy's name was Spartacus. During this period, the Romans were desperate to expand their growing empire. As a result, the Romans captured millions of slaves and forced them into back-breaking work. Slaves smashed rocks in mines, toiled in fields, and rowed galley ships—all for the great glory and benefit of Rome. Because Spartacus was strong and healthy, he was drafted into the army to help defend and expand Rome's territories.

According to the Greek philosopher Plutarch, Spartacus was brought to Rome as a slave along with his wife and other members of his Thracian tribe. On his first night in Rome, a snake slithered along the ground towards Spartacus while he slept. His wife woke up and saw the serpent coiled around her husband's face, but instead of being afraid, she saw the snake as an omen: a fearsome power that would one day lead her husband to doom or glory.

Not one to follow orders, Spartacus ran away from the army but was later caught and imprisoned. A brief taste of freedom shut out by the clang of chains. As punishment, Spartacus was charged with desertion and sold to a gladiator school where he was forced to swear an oath of allegiance: "To be burned, to be bound, to be beaten, to be killed, and to obey his master without question." Ever since his capture, Spartacus had been forced to fight and spill blood for Rome. Now he wanted nothing more than to escape the chains that bound him and reclaim his freedom.

While enduring harsh conditions and intense training, Spartacus plotted his escape. In 73 BC, he made his move. Convincing seventy other slaves to join him, Spartacus led a revolt against the gladiator school. Rushing into the kitchens, the slaves grabbed utensils and fought their way out of the *ludus*. Spartacus and his rebel slaves were no longer fighting to entertain Rome; they were fighting for their freedom.

The rebellion captivated Rome and was so inspiring that Spartacus's small band of gladiators soon grew to more than 120,000 slaves. No longer a foot soldier, Spartacus now stood at the head of an army that fought to escape the tyranny of the Roman Empire. Spartacus knew it was better to die free than live in chains. And while he would ultimately meet his death fighting against Rome, Spartacus's quest for freedom liberated thousands of slaves, driving a stake through the heart of the Roman Empire. In Spartacus's case, the prophecy delivered by the serpent was not glory or death, but glory and death.

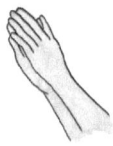

Slavery ends with destruction, which turns to creation, and, if nurtured correctly, develops into mastery. Here, mastery refers to mastery of the self, mastery of your environment, mastery of time, and mastery of your life. You're no longer a slave to your thoughts and behaviors. And instead of falling victim to dysfunctional beliefs, you take control of your life. But this is no easy task. Mastery is challenging for one simple reason: It requires complete and brutal honesty.

Complete mastery means taking control of your life and setting yourself on the path to freedom. It also means staying true to reality. In your search for the truth on the path to enlightenment, awareness is the first step. You understand which negative thoughts and behaviors hold you back, and you take active steps to destroy them. All this requires conscious effort and discipline.

While discipline might appear to be restrictive, there is, counterintuitively, great freedom in discipline. Socrates, the Ancient Greek philosopher, once said: "The truly free individual is only free to the extent of his self-mastery." Those who don't govern themselves are condemned to be governed by others. To avoid enslavement, you must exercise discipline and control. If you want better health, you must have the discipline to exercise. If you want to lose weight, you must have the discipline to eat the right type of food. If you want financial freedom, you must have the discipline to take control of your spending. And if you want the freedom to live life on your own terms, you must have the discipline to make your own decisions.

When life plunges you into chaos, discipline is the hand that reaches down and pulls you from despair. Thus, the more disciplined you are, the more mastery and freedom you achieve. You must not allow your pursuit of immediate gratification to control your life. You no longer play the victim, responding to the whims of your emotions. Instead, you take control of your destiny and master your emotions.

It is, of course, easier to eat junk food than healthy meals, just as it's easier to stay in a comfortable job than to start a new business or career. It's also easier to avoid life's problems and emotional pain by escaping into addiction. People often embrace addiction to escape their emotional pain. They pursue alcohol, drugs, food, and pleasure, but no amount of escape can dull their pain.

When we try to bury our feelings and run from the past, we become vulnerable and leave ourselves open to the perils of addiction. And no matter how hard we try to escape, we can only hide from our problems for so long. If you're unable to master your emotions, you are likely to experience mass internal conflict and turmoil—turmoil that only gets worse as you drift further away from your authentic self and split in two.

Master Your Emotions

"Rule your mind, or it will rule you."

– Horace

Emotions are crucial because they enable us to appreciate and enjoy life. Without emotion, you wouldn't be able to feel joy and delight, just as you wouldn't be able to experience suffering and despair. Your emotions are not only the means through which you experience life; they also fuel your thoughts. We use the power of thought to make plans, analyze situations, learn new information, and solve problems. But thoughts by themselves have no energy or power. And without energy, our thoughts disappear into thin air.

Consider the following situation. A man is excited by the idea of starting a new weight-loss program. He thinks about all the ways his life will improve once he loses weight. He knows for a fact that he'll feel healthier, happier, and more confident about himself. This thought alone provides hope for the future.

Now, consider another man, weighed down by negative thinking, who's considering the same weight-loss program. When he thinks about losing weight, he feels depressed and upset. He thinks about all the food he can't eat and how uncomfortable his life will become. His despair causes him to lose motivation and desire. There's no emotional fuel left in the tank. And without emotional fuel, the man has no energy to turn his thoughts into reality.

Emotions are more than just a measure of how you feel. They are a source of infinite energy, providing you with the essential fuel you need to grow and develop. This is why it's so important to cultivate the right emotions. If you spend most of your time lost in a haze of negative emotions, your energy levels will crash, and you'll have no motivation to take action. Sometimes you might wonder why you feel tired and have no energy. People who work in jobs that require little mental or physical effort can still feel exhausted by lunchtime. This type of exhaustion is known as emotional fatigue.

Emotional fatigue can make you feel tired even if you aren't exerting yourself. It is much more debilitating than physical or mental fatigue. For example, your job might cause you to feel a slew of negative emotions, ranging from boredom to frustration to despair. These emotions can leave you feeling empty and depleted. You have no energy left in the tank. In this respect, our emotions are like a nuclear reactor. If managed with care, they provide us with a limitless supply of energy. On the other hand, if most of our emotions are negative, leaking poison into our nuclear core, we deprive our body of vital energy and soon run out of steam. Emotions such as stress, depression, anxiety, worry, and despair leave us feeling depleted and run-down. In contrast, emotions such as hope, gratitude, curiosity, interest, and love are all abundant sources of energy.

Nevertheless, if you're unable to manage your emotions—a common trait of the emotional slave—your emotions will continue to disrupt your thoughts and control your behavior. While you attempt to gain mastery over your life, it's easy to slip back into the role of a slave as you struggle to shake off certain thoughts and beliefs. Not having control over your emotions prevents healthy and accurate decision-making. Painful emotions and unhealthy attachments also limit your ability to live a life of abundance and prosperity.

John, an ambitious man in his mid-thirties, is struggling to overcome an unhealthy attachment to his girlfriend. John's situation is not unique. In fact, it's all too common. John claims to be head over heels in love with Eve, a woman he met at work. Even though they've only been dating for two weeks, John is consumed by worry. He is worried that Eve doesn't love him the way he loves her; that she will think he isn't good enough for her; and that she will one day leave him for someone else. Even the name Eve bothers him. Didn't Eve seduce Adam? Fuck! Maybe she'll try to seduce someone in the office.

There isn't a day that goes by when John doesn't wonder if he's losing his mind. To soothe his anxiety, he tells Eve he doesn't want her talking to other men. And, as an extra condition, he wants her to check in with him every couple of hours and share her location. Finally, to overcome his fear that Eve will leave him, John love-bombs Eve with flowers and expensive gifts in a futile attempt to win her over. John's love is the worst kind of all: possessive and controlling instead of freeing and supportive.

Suffering occurs when expectation collides with reality. Thus, to free yourself from suffering, you must first free yourself from expectation. Suppose you hold the belief that everyone should be nice. When you discover that's not the case, your expectation is shattered, and you suffer as a result. Likewise, if you hold the expectation that you should be happy, you'll experience suffering and torment when you encounter painful emotions and setbacks.

Suppose a woman is on the receiving end of a nasty comment. If she is a slave to her emotions, the nasty comment will cut deep. Anytime anyone says anything to upset her, she'll feel disrespected and hurt. And the more she dwells upon the situation, the angrier she'll become.

Now consider another woman who is in control of her emotions in the same situation. She might feel upset or hurt by a nasty comment, but she doesn't let her anger consume her. Instead of seething, searching for a way to get revenge, she leans into her emotional pain, feels her anger, and makes a conscious decision to let go.

Instead of holding on to painful emotions and unhealthy attachments, you can make an active choice to let them go. If you feel a well of anger rise up inside you whenever you think about a nasty comment someone once said to you, it's your choice to decide whether you want to feed that rage or release it. Learning how to let go of painful feelings puts you in control instead of making you a slave to your emotions.

It's tempting to feel anger towards people and situations that make you upset. But anytime you feel a painful emotion, it's a good idea to steady yourself, take a deep breath, and ask yourself why you're feeling this way. Why do you feel angry, frustrated, or upset? Has someone said something that struck a nerve or exposed a vulnerable side of your personality?

If someone calls you stupid, does this insult shake you to the core? Do you keep thinking about the insult and the person who upset you? How dare they call you stupid when they're more stupid than you! You feel a hot flush of anger course through your body. *I'll show them*, you tell yourself. *I'll get them back. I'll make them fucking hurt, just like they hurt me!* Your emotions continue to run amok, creating turmoil and further fueling your anger.

Instead of leaning into your anger, it's more effective to ask why being called stupid upsets you so much? You're not stupid, so why does an insult like this bother you? Is it because it conflicts with the belief that you're smarter and more intelligent than other people? Has this person triggered your ego's defense mechanism? Before you let go of your anger, it might be a good idea to ask yourself whether your ego is functioning in a healthy way or if it is unbalanced and over-inflated?

The ego is present in all humans and is as unique and distinctive as our individual personalities. So what is the ego, and why is it so damaging? The ego is a construction of your thoughts, emotions, beliefs, and experiences. It is your identity. It's how you identify with yourself. If a person is labeled egocentric, they are self-centered. This is because the ego is, by its very nature, selfish. It is there, not to ensure your happiness and peace of mind, but to ensure your survival. With this in mind, the ego cares only about one thing—building itself up, getting stronger, getting better, and getting more powerful.

Like a monster with a ravenous appetite, the ego is never satisfied. It wants more possessions, more attention, more fame, more money, and more status. In addition, the ego seeks validation by identifying with certain beliefs, people, objects, and possessions to further inflate itself and grow stronger. For example, when a person buys luxury goods, they are not just buying a product, they are associating themselves with a brand's image. This identification makes a person feel more sophisticated and prestigious, which, in turn, feeds the ego and its need to feel superior to other people. In extreme situations, the ego can make us believe we are someone we are not and lose touch with reality. If your ego is unbalanced, you're likely to experience emotional volatility whenever you feel threatened.

An insecure ego is full of shame and insecurity, while an over-inflated ego exudes narcissism and grandiosity. If you tell yourself that you're the most intelligent person in the world and better than everyone else, your ego will naturally become over-inflated. The more you try to build yourself up, the more vulnerable you are to attack. Just as a bloated ego is easy to burst, the person who strips away their ego by removing deluded self-beliefs becomes immune to attack.

The master recognizes the ego for what it is: a spoiled, petulant child. If you wish to reduce your ego and the influence it has on your life, you must first become aware of its existence. Like a creature that shies away from the light, the ego shies away from awareness. A healthy ego is resistant to attack, insults, and setbacks.

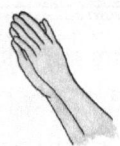

Ganesh, the Hindu god with the head of an elephant, teaches his followers to avoid ego and arrogance and instead cultivate wisdom. For, without wisdom, power is ruthless, and mastery turns to enslavement. When your ego is balanced, compliments and insults no longer affect you because you've lost interest in feeding your ego. So, what is the best way to cultivate a healthy ego?

The first way to reduce your ego and balance your emotions is to practice gratitude. The second method is to practice mindfulness. Gratitude teaches us to be thankful for what we have. We learn to appreciate the people around us and the many small blessings that come into our life. Gratitude has the power to transform the way we look at the world. Through gratitude, we learn to appreciate life.

While a person might consider themselves unlucky if they compare themselves to someone who lived fifty years ago, there's a strong argument that there has never been a better time to be alive. We have entertainment on demand, the ability to travel anywhere in the world, access to medicine, the freedom to choose how to live, information and knowledge at our fingertips, and an overabundance of food.

We often forget these facts, however, as we spend most of our time comparing ourselves to other people. We forget how lucky we are and fail to notice all the small blessings in our life: a comfortable bed, a nutritious meal, good friends, freedom of choice, a healthy body, and a safe living environment. We become fixated on what we don't have, and, in the process, suck the joy out of life. Life becomes serious, an all-or-nothing game where the stakes are win or lose, succeed or fail, live or die.

If we take a moment to think about all the ridiculous plans we've made, all the grand posturing, and petty moments of jealousy, we can gain a real sense of perspective over our life. Laughter is a magical tonic. And when we laugh at ourselves, this has the wonderful effect of balancing the ego and exposing the shadow self. Besides cultivating gratitude, mindfulness is another useful technique that helps keep the ego in check and balance our emotions.

Mindfulness is a type of meditation that brings awareness to our thoughts. Instead of judging our thoughts, we let them pass through us without judgment and without filter. During mindfulness meditation, you might notice that your thoughts come rushing out, tripping over each other, jumping from one idea to the next without meaning or cohesion.

You might feel as though your mind is chaotic and restless. Nevertheless, you mustn't shy away from your thoughts. Instead, you must allow them to pass through you. You are simply a witness to your thoughts. Then, when the disorder and chaos within your mind subsides, you'll notice certain pain points and problem areas keep rising to the surface. Only then, through conscious effort and awareness, can you work through your thoughts, learn valuable lessons, and let unnecessary emotions go.

Master Your Fear

"We suffer more in imagination than in reality."

– Seneca

Are you scared of the future? Are you afraid that you'll fail to live up to your expectations? Are you worried about your life, your relationships, your career? Where does all this anxiety and worry come from? If you examine the root cause of humanity's suffering, you'll see the same monster reappear time and time again—that monster is fear. Getting control of your life means moving forward despite feeling anxiety and fear. You cannot, however, run away from fear because it is faster than you. The only way to overcome fear is to confront it head-on.

Marie Curie, the Nobel Prize-winning scientist who discovered radium and polonium, once said: "Nothing in life is to be feared. It is only to be understood. Now is the time to understand more so that you may fear less." While Marie Curie made a series of incredible scientific discoveries, what is even more remarkable is that she made them amidst great tragedy and depression.

After losing both her mother and sister at an early age, Marie collapsed into a deep, year-long depression. Upon graduating from school, hardship followed Marie to Paris, where she lived in poverty in a small room with no heating and barely enough food to eat. Despite these setbacks, she won two Nobel Prizes and prolonged the lives of millions of cancer patients around the world.

It takes great courage to act when you feel paralyzed, to push through resistance, and to move forward despite your fear. Fear is guaranteed to rear its ugly head whenever you try to change your life or make a big decision. It's as though fear is challenging you to back down. It takes courage to end a relationship, to walk out of a job, to move to a different country, to change career, or accept that you're on the wrong path.

You feel fear because finding a new path means moving towards an uncertain future. Fear will always be there, but fear exists only in the mind. If you believe that fear is holding you back, preventing you from moving forward, you must acknowledge this fact before taking steps to destroy your fear.

An extreme example of someone mastering fear is the diver who, without the protection of a cage, jumps into the water and swims with great white sharks. These fearsome predators, which can grow to more than 20 feet long and weigh more than a ton, excel at hunting. Despite its notoriety, the great white plays a vital role in the world's ecosystem. Nevertheless, it is also responsible for more human fatalities than any other shark. The great white is all the more terrifying because of the way it hunts, hiding in the shadows before appearing from out of nowhere in a flash of teeth and muscle.

So how does a diver slip into the water and summon the courage to swim with great white sharks? The answer is both unexpected and counterintuitive. The diver must swim towards the shark instead of away from it. If you saw a great white shark, how would you react? Most people would either freeze in terror or swim away as fast as possible. In this case, our fear destroys us before the shark even has a chance to sink its teeth into us.

When you run away from your fear—the way seals swim away from sharks—fear catches up to you and destroys you. Fear expects you to run away. It expects you to be the easy victim, just as the great white expects its prey to swim in the opposite direction. Once you summon the courage to face your fear, however, and swim towards the shark, fear evaporates. You discover that fear is nothing more than an abstract illusion created by the mind.

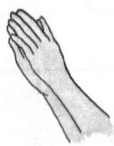

In the same way that rocks turn into diamonds, humans also develop and grow stronger under extreme pressure. We must not shy away from fear; instead, we must use it to motivate us to take action. On the other hand, if you allow fear to overwhelm you, your life will be half-lived, crippled, and riddled with regret. You'll fail to get the love you crave, the work you deserve, and the life you desire. This is why it's so important to confront fear head-on.

Master Your Truth

"No one saves us but ourselves."

– Buddha

A young mother is trapped in a loveless marriage in a foreign country. Far from home and with no money to support herself and her infant daughter, the woman knows she must change her life or remain trapped in a relationship that stifles her existence. Desperate for change, the woman makes the tough decision to pack her belongings and return home with her baby girl. At this juncture in her life, the woman feels like a complete failure. Her life is a mess, her marriage is over, and she has no job or income to support herself. Everything she's worked so hard to build—her relationship, her family, and her life—is now in ruins.

Returning home to a life of poverty and little in the way of support, the woman contemplates suicide, calling her life at that moment "as poor as it's possible to be without being homeless." At such a low point, it would have been easy for the woman to give up. Instead, driven by a mixture of hope and desperation, the woman does the only thing she can when all she has left in the world is an "old typewriter and a big idea"—she begins to write.

The woman writes in cafes, at home, and anywhere she can between struggling to survive and taking care of her daughter. In the woman's own words: "I stopped pretending to myself that I was anything other than what I was, and began to direct all my energy to finishing the only work that mattered to me." Rock bottom was now a solid foundation on which to rebuild her life. The woman understood that the moment she followed her purpose, her creativity and courage would propel her towards freedom and security. At that moment, trapped between poverty and despair, the woman had no idea that she would go on to become one of the bestselling authors in history.

False beliefs obscure the path to freedom. Instead of deluding yourself, you mustn't be afraid to acknowledge your faults and insecurities, for honesty is the surest path to freedom. There's no shame in acknowledging that you're on the wrong path. You must, however, have the courage to admit this to yourself. We must never ignore our inner truth. Instead, we must shine a light on the dark parts of our soul. Only then, in a moment of complete honesty, can we break the chains that bind us and escape our enslavement.

If you discover that a part of you is fractured, and you're not as whole as you once thought, this is a sign that you need to reconnect with your authentic self. We become fractured when we deny who we are and ignore our inner truth. We become lost and directionless, like a ship without a rudder drifting on the open ocean. We lose touch with our authentic self, allowing other people, events, and situations to become our master.

Many people live lives that conflict with their true purpose and core beliefs. A man struggling to become an actor is inauthentic when his only aim is to become rich and famous. Does he really want to become an actor? The answer is no. If you asked the man to tell you his true passion, he'd say health and fitness. Acting simply appealed to his ego's desire for fame and recognition. You might want society and people to respect you. But this desire for recognition will force you onto a path of misery. It will force you to do things you don't want to do and live a life you don't want to live.

We see this in the story of Phil, a married man who walked out on his wife for no apparent reason and without explanation. When Phil left everything behind, the question on everyone's lips was, "How could a man walk out on his wife and kids and disappear into thin air?" The answer: twenty years of inauthentic living. Phil had been reluctant to marry his wife in the first place, and he only committed to the marriage because he thought it was the right thing to do.

While Phil cared for his wife (more for sentimental reasons than anything else), their relationship had never been free-flowing and easy. The years ticked by, and Phil grew increasingly frustrated. Yet, he chose to stay in the marriage and have children out of a strong sense of obligation and a desire to fit in. After all, he didn't want to make his wife unhappy or appear out of place when all his friends and coworkers were happily married.

Now, after twenty years, Phil hated his job, resented his wife, and believed his son and daughter were old enough to handle any difficulties that might arise from his sudden departure. It was all too much, Phil thought as he made plans to start a new life somewhere else. Yet, he only had himself to blame—he knew that much. Phil wished he could go back in time and start life all over again. Given a second chance, he would live life on his own terms. He would marry a woman he loved, pursue a job he was passionate about, and have children when he was ready.

Could I really have a second chance? Phil wondered. *A chance to do things my way? It's probably too late. My life is already fucked. But the longer I stay in this life, the more fucked up I'll become, and the more miserable I'll make everyone else.* This thought was the catalyst for a psychological disturbance that shook Phil to his core. In Phil's mind, the only way he could make everything right was to leave it all behind and start over again.

Phil's actions would be felt far and wide, impacting his wife, his children, his family, and his friends. Of course, to everyone except Phil, his disappearance was an act of extreme selfishness. The act of a man who only thought about himself. But this sentiment was only half true. Phil's disappearance was a desperate attempt to correct a life that had veered so far off course, he no longer knew who he was or how he'd come to be in this situation. All Phil knew was that ignoring his instincts had led him down the wrong path. Now, all he wanted was to escape from his marriage and reclaim his freedom.

Here's a hard truth: If you don't control your life, other people and events will become your master. You must have the courage to make your own decisions. Otherwise, other people will make decisions for you and steer your life in the wrong direction. It takes great resolve to live an authentic life because that means taking risks and sometimes upsetting the people you love. Even more terrifying is the knowledge that living an authentic life often means hurting ourselves. The pain of an authentic life, however, is short. But the pain of an inauthentic life is long and drawn-out, causing endless suffering to ourselves and others.

All humans seek to maximize pleasure and avoid pain. It's uncomfortable to look at our life and see all our mistakes and bad decisions laid out before us. For this reason, we often try to avoid painful situations and emotions. But by doing so, we make our lives that much more difficult in the long run.

Emotional avoidance is like putting your hand in a fire and expecting not to get burnt. When you put your hand in a fire, the pain acts as a warning signal to keep you safe. You remember the pain, so you avoid sticking your hand in any more fires. But if you ignore the warning signal, you will keep getting burnt until your hand becomes damaged beyond repair. The same is true of emotional pain. If you go through life trying to avoid uncomfortable emotions, you'll never learn life's important lessons, and you'll condemn yourself to repeat the same mistakes over and over again.

For the past six years, Mia has struggled to cope with her own form of emotional pain. Trapped in an abusive marriage with a man who doesn't respect her, Mia wants nothing more than to end her suffering. So why does she continue to stay in a loveless marriage? She hopes that one day her husband will change and love her the way he promised to love her when they first met. Despite the abuse, Mia clings to the belief that her husband is a wonderful man, having seen glimpses of his love when they first began dating. But it doesn't matter how long Mia waits or how much she prays, her husband doesn't change. In fact, he only gets worse.

What started out as a beautiful relationship is now a broken, loveless marriage that should have ended years ago. Despite Mia's doubt and uncertainty, she tries to convince herself that her husband is still in love with her. *He just has trouble expressing his feelings*, she tells herself for the hundredth time after recovering from another round of abuse. Thus, when Mia's marriage comes crashing down after another explosive fight, she's overwhelmed with grief but not surprised. Mia's grief, however, is not for the loss of the relationship but the loss of a love that never existed. You can only deny the truth for so long.

Life is an endless cycle of destruction and creation where the end goal is not completion but growth. "One should never think that man can reach perfection," wrote Carl Jung, the founder of analytical psychology. "He can only aim at completion—not to be perfect but to be complete." Within the endless cycle of creation and destruction, you must remain true to your inner voice and pursue your purpose with passion and zeal. When you resist your calling and move away from your purpose, you deny yourself and the world your greatest gifts.

The Roman philosopher Epictetus once told his followers: "Stick with your purpose. Do not seek external approval. Do not worry about anything outside of your control. The only things you command are your thoughts and actions. You choose your response. Stop aspiring to be anyone other than your own best self and your truth, for that does fall within your control."

When you follow your purpose, you become one with the universe, and a powerful force awakens within. This life force works in the background to help you achieve your goals. Whether you call this mysterious force an angel or spirit guide, this force is more powerful and benevolent than we realize. If you listen closely, you'll hear your spirit guide tell you which path to follow and which paths to avoid. Sometimes your spirit voice will be loud and clear, and at other times, you'll hear just a whisper, almost like a sixth sense. Listen, and your purpose will become clear.

If your inner voice tells you to climb a mountain, learn to surf, paint, start a family, stay single, or create a business, pay close attention. This is your inner truth. Ignore it and you'll soon find yourself back on the wrong path, a path filled with frustration and despair. The universe rewards those who take the right path and punishes those who cling to the wrong one. When you align with the truth, you align with the universe. By following your true purpose, you serve the universe, and the universe rewards you in return.

A man who dreams of designing and building furniture suffers at the hands of the universe when he stays in an insignificant job he despises. The man's health, mind, and creativity suffer. The moment the man takes control of his life, destroying the path he's on to become a furniture maker, something incredible happens: his health improves, his mind becomes energized, his creativity explodes, and his income skyrockets. When you become a master of your passion, instead of a slave in an industry you care nothing about, the universe rewards you. You no longer serve yourself by pursuing wealth, recognition, and pleasure with reckless abandon. Instead, you serve the universe by pursuing your true purpose.

If you choose to live a life of greed and self-interest, you live in direct conflict with the universe. Instead, you should work with the common collective truths passed down from generation to generation that are part of humanity's subconscious. These include god, energy, sacrifice, health, well-being, longevity, and environmental preservation. Whether these truths are represented by Jesus, Muhammed, Buddha, Zeus, or Vishnu, the energy that binds humanity together is founded on love and gratitude—gratitude for ourselves, for others, and for our environment.

Suppose you choose to live a life devoid of love and gratitude. In that case, you move in direct opposition to the universe. If you want love, you must give love. If you want financial freedom, you must provide value to others. If you want respect, you must earn it. Only when you embrace these simple truths can you move on to a higher level of growth.

You receive the truth of the universe the moment you're born. The great universal truths are encoded into your DNA and passed down from one generation to the next. The mental models we receive are often so powerful they determine our life trajectory. Despite receiving these collective truths from the universe, our mental models are also influenced by the belief system we inherit from our parents, peers, and society. This can explain why children from wealthy families often find it so easy to make money and why children from low-income families find it so difficult to escape the poverty trap.

The child from a rich family receives the right mental model for accumulating wealth. They learn how to deal with risk and how to invest their money. In contrast, the child from a low-income family learns to avoid risk and grows up with the belief that success is out of their reach. Their mental model tells them to stay in their lane, keep their head down, and be grateful for any job that puts food on the table.

Aristotle touched on this when he said: "Show me the child at seven, and I will show you the man." This quote demonstrates how difficult it is to change our beliefs. If you wish to create change, you must first make the unconscious conscious by bringing your old beliefs into the light. Only then, in a moment of stark exposure, can you start to question your beliefs, assessing the impact each dysfunctional belief has on your life. You might ask yourself which beliefs are valid, and if your beliefs connect with the truth of the universe? In the same way that studies show newborn babies are imprinted with a fear of snakes, we're imprinted with the truth of the universe the moment we're born. We intuitively understand the difference between right and wrong, good and evil, love and hate.

During the first seven years of life, a child experiences vigorous theta activity in the brain. Here, theta activity refers to a slow frequency of between four and seven hertz that puts the mind into an almost hypnotic state. High theta activity is associated with higher levels of intuition, creativity, daydreaming, and the storage of memories, emotions, and sensations. When we grow older, however, our theta activity declines, which reduces our ability to be intuitive and creative. The only time adults have high theta activity is during periods of sleep, meditation, and hypnosis.

Part of the reason why children find it so easy to learn new information is because they have higher levels of theta activity. A child's mind is like a sponge ready to soak up new information from the universe. When your theta activity is high, your mind is in the perfect state to receive new information. This information includes basic functions such as how to stay safe and how to interact with the world.

While a lot of the information we receive is beneficial, we also receive a lot of negative information in the form of dysfunctional beliefs and bad mental models. These dysfunctional beliefs and bad mental models derail us at best and enslave us at worst. We often receive debilitating information from our parents, teachers, peers, and society. This is why it's so important to cut negative information out of our life before it derails us and sends us too far down the wrong path.

One way to access a theta state and encourage new beliefs is to use meditation or hypnosis to open up new neural pathways in the brain. When you lose your way and don't know which path to take, sometimes you must go back to your childhood to find yourself. For example, suppose you spent a lot of time painting and drawing as a child. Even though you haven't done anything creative for the past twenty years, your creative urge is still there, beating inside you. It can never be silenced, no matter how hard you try to suppress it. Now, as an adult, you notice that your inner voice keeps calling out to you, desperate to reconnect with your artistic spirit.

Similarly, perhaps you spent your childhood playing in the ocean, thinking about all the wonderful marine life under the water. Now, as you sit at your desk, you notice that the ocean keeps calling out to you. You dream of its beauty, vastness, and depth, and crave the feeling of water on your skin. The ocean rests at the heart of your primal core, calling out for connection. Stray too far from your primal core, the part of you that connects with the universe, and it's natural to feel lost and malnourished, as though stranded in a desert without water.

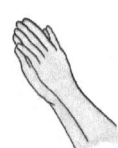

It's not uncommon to wake up one day and feel upset at the way life has turned out. It's easy for us to lose our way and find ourselves on the wrong path. Sometimes you might look in the mirror and wonder where you went wrong. It might feel as though you're looking at the reflection of someone who missed every opportunity that came their way—and you're not alone. Indeed, many people wonder why they feel dissatisfied and unhappy with the direction of their life.

Many people labor under the delusion that they're in charge of their destiny. Yet, they have little to no control over anything that happens. When you realize that your beliefs conflict with your primal core and the collective truths of the universe, you're likely to experience mass internal conflict and disruption. The only way to avoid internal destruction is to honor the truth and become one with the universe. You must reject all forms of slavery. In doing so, you once more gain control over your life and move towards a path of vitality, prosperity, and freedom.